THE PHOENIX PROJECT

Rebirth and Reinvention
A Career Change Playbook for Women Over 50

CLAIRE MOFFAT

First published by Ultimate World Publishing 2026
Copyright © 2026 Claire Moffat

ISBN

Paperback: 978-1-923583-75-7
Ebook: 978-1-923583-76-4

Cover design: Ultimate World Publishing
Layout and typesetting: Ultimate World Publishing
Editor: Nora Williamson
Cover Image Copyright: aleksej015-Shutterstock.com

Ultimate World Publishing
Diamond Creek,
Victoria Australia 3089
www.writeabook.com.au

About the Author

Claire Moffat is a writer, career coach, and digital-media pioneer, passionate about helping women over 50 design meaningful and financially confident next chapters. She was one of the initial students to graduate from the first BA in Communication, majoring in Journalism in Australia. In her mid-twenties she became an investigative journalist for Fairfax and Sons weekly newspaper, The National Times.

In her thirties she became the first female group business publisher at The Yaffa Group, then Australia's largest private B2B publisher and by her forties she had created connectedaustralia.com, Australia's first daily digital B2B news platform for the global consumer electronics industry.

At fifty, Claire founded connectedwomen.net.au, the world's first technology news site for women.

After decades as a business journalist and editor, digital media pioneer and mentor to women in career transition, Claire has written The Phoenix Project to empower female midlife reinvention through mindset, strategy and story. She lives in Sydney, Australia, where she continues to guide women to rise, rebuild and thrive.

Testimonials

I worked with Claire throughout 2018, and learned how to set goals that are in alignment with my values and dreams, which I then proceeded to take action towards. Claire kept me accountable and on the path I wanted to go. Claire brings a depth of experience, warmth, and compassion to her coaching style. She gently but firmly guided me to the next action I needed to take. I found the monthly sessions insightful and very much looked forward to my meetings with Claire.

Sharon McKinney, Associate Director, Station Lead Estimator

I always enjoyed my sessions with Claire. She's very insightful and can explain things that I sort of knew but couldn't articulate. She picked up negative traits that I didn't realise were negative. She's honest.

Susie O'Sullivan, Finance Specialist

Claire provided the roadmap and encouragement to allow me to get out of my 'comfort zone' to speak up within my industry through utilising social media, traditional print media, and even television! Within a year, I was blogging for Women's Network Australia with 20,000 members, was an expert commentator on SBS World News on trademarks and was even quoted in a Sydney Morning Herald article.

**Binh Rey, General Manager Trade Mark Attorney
with Branding Expertise**

Claire is an amazing speaker and coach. I first approached Claire with no idea of how to utilize LinkedIn. Through private coaching combined with her four-week LinkedIn Mastery Course, Claire took me on an incredible journey of discovering my 'Why', building a personal brand. And transformed the way I use and communicate on LinkedIn.

Impressed by the transformation, Claire was invited to speak at my organisation; Professional Development Forum where she gave an open and practical talk on how to create a personal brand. The event was a great success where she recorded the most number of ticket sales for a single speaker. Feedback for her event was fantastic. To quote one of our guests, "I was totally inspired, have new insight and a mission to accomplish."

Victoria Chun, Startup Business Consultant and Project Manager

Dedication

For my mother, who always had faith in me
and Dr Brian Gutkin who reminded me,
again and again, that I had a book worth writing.

Contents

INTRODUCTION

A New Chapter Begins: Writing the Life You Want, One Bold Page at a Time

It was a fresh May morning in 2013, and I was in my Sydney office on Market Street when the phone rang. A familiar wave of anxiety washed over me — though truthfully, it was closer to dread. My 13-year-old company, Connected Digital Media, was bleeding money, and the creditors were beginning to circle.

My accountant's name flashed on the screen. I prayed that it would be good news.

It wasn't.

Warwick didn't waste time with small talk. His voice was serious, yet compassionate as he delivered the news: the enormous debt the ATO was demanding wasn't mine. It was unpaid PAYG tax, quietly accumulated over several years and buried within the company accounts. Myself and my ex-husband were company directors and somehow, my solicitor, the head of family law at the large firm I trusted to perform due diligence, hadn't checked my ex-husband's accounts when she advised me to buy the business from him.

Like so many women of my generation, I had handed over the financial reins of our business without question. You trust your father, so you trust your husband. It felt almost written into the vows.

When I signed the property settlement in December 2012, I owned a thriving digital media company, Connected Digital Media, turning over $800,000 a year, with a 15% profit margin and blue-chip advertisers. I had no debt, owned my home outright, and held healthy cash reserves and superannuation.

By April 2014, less than a year after that phone call, it was all gone. No income. No home. $30,000 in debt. At 58, I had become one of Australia's most invisible statistics: an older homeless woman.

I had crossed into a parallel Sydney— one that coexisted with the world of comfort and confidence I'd known, yet operated under entirely different rules. One where I was totally unprepared.

The months that followed blurred into confusion and grief. Each day felt like wading through quicksand, searching for footing that no longer existed. How could this happen in Australia, to someone like me? The betrayal ran deep: personal, professional, systemic.

Every path forward seemed blocked. Without money for a barrister, I couldn't pursue legal action. I felt powerless.

> How could a woman who had built a global business, led teams, and negotiated complex contracts end up here? By day, shame wrapped around me, by night, fear for my future wouldn't let me sleep.

My next steps

It took around 18 months for me to even think about getting back on my feet. I hadn't worked for an employer for almost 15 years and I was now 60.

Instead of heading back into the highly-pressured world of B2B publishing, I began training as a coach, a good choice for my communication skillset and it was a micro business that I could develop at my own pace. By focusing on helping others succeed, I was able to get some relief from ruminating on my circumstances, and gradually, I was able to start putting a new life together for myself. It seemed the more I helped others, the more my pain began to heal.

People would often say, "You should write a book." For years I resisted, but as I continued to work with other women in their 50s, I realized that my story was not unusual. Many had faced similar setbacks: divorce, financial loss, redundancy, health challenges, or the quiet erosion of confidence after decades of giving themselves to others. Again and again, I heard the same question: "Is it too late for me?"

Here's the truth I learned the hardest way possible: it is never too late.

Like the proverbial phoenix rising from the ashes, I eventually found my footing. It took years of rebuilding, of trial and error, of humbling myself to start again from almost nothing. It took courage I didn't know I had. And it took a belief, sometimes faint, that the best years of my life were not over.

If anything, it was just beginning.

The New Power Decade: How Women Over 50 Are Reinventing Work

When you hit 50, something shifts. For many women, it feels as if the world quietly begins to whisper that you're "past your prime." Workplaces may subtly suggest it's time to step aside for younger talent. Society celebrates youth, beauty, and energy, while overlooking wisdom, resilience, and experience.

My experience has been that success has no age limit. As I sit here writing this, I'm into my seventh decade.

The story of your career is not finished. In fact, for many women, the years after 50 are the most powerful, creative, and fulfilling chapter of all.

At this stage of life, you have the freedom, experience, and courage to create your own version of success, one that is deeply personal and far more satisfying than a job title on a business card. For many women, midlife is the moment to pivot from working for others' approval to working with purpose. Success is no longer about chasing promotions or clocking long hours; it's about choosing work that feels meaningful, flexible, and aligned with your values.

The beauty of reaching this stage is the wealth of skills and wisdom you bring. You've navigated challenges, built resilience, and learned how to adapt. These qualities make you a natural leader, mentor, or innovator. Far from slowing down, this is often the season when women step into their fullest power.

Why Your Biggest Challenges Aren't Stopping You—They're Shaping You

Stepping into a new chapter of work and success after 50 comes with unique challenges. Ageism is real. Confidence gaps can hold women back. Technology changes fast. These hurdles are undeniable, but they are not immovable.

I know this because I have lived there. When I lost everything, I also lost my sense of self-worth. I wondered if the business world had passed me by, if I was too old to start again. But step by step, I discovered that the very qualities that come with age, resilience, clarity, and perspective, are the same qualities that help us thrive in the second half of life.

Think about it: by 50, you've already faced setbacks, losses, and reinventions. You know what it takes to rise. You have grit. You have perspective. And most importantly, you have a choice.

Your Secret Weapon Isn't Youth—It's Wisdom

One of the greatest gifts of being over 50 is wisdom. Decades of living and working give you a perspective that no degree or title can match. You can cut through noise, see the bigger picture, and make decisions with empathy and clarity. These are the qualities the world needs now more than ever.

Your experience is another asset. You've adapted to change, solved problems, and built relationships across industries and communities. Those connections and insights are your currency. Don't underestimate their value.

And perhaps most importantly, you have resilience. Life has tested you, and you're still here. That grit gives you the courage to try new things and the strength to keep going when obstacles appear.

The Promise of this Book

Here's the promise I want you to hold onto as you step into these pages: it is absolutely possible to build a career after 50 that feels fulfilling, financially secure, and aligned with who you are today.

This book is not about starting from scratch; it's about building on everything you've already achieved. It's about redefining success on your terms, because you've already lived a full, rich life. Now it's your time to create work that reflects your values, your strengths, and your dreams.

Maybe you're craving more freedom. Perhaps you want to finally use your talents in a way that feels meaningful. Or maybe financial independence is your priority, so you can step into the years ahead with confidence. Whatever your goals, this book will help you design a career that works for you.

By the end of this journey, you won't just see what's possible. You'll have the tools and confidence to make it happen.

Your next chapter can be your best chapter yet.

PART ONE

Resetting Your Mindset

1

The Forgotten Generation Finds Its Voice: Why Gen X Women Are Ready to Rewrite Midlife

If we were to create an avatar of a woman on the verge of 50, we need look no further than women born between 1965 and 1980 known as Generation X.

It has sometimes been called the 'middle child' generation, as it follows the well-known baby boomer generation (1945-1965) and precedes the millennials (born 1981– 1996). Generation X has also been called the 'baby bust' generation. Its members were born when the high birth rates of the baby boomer decades declined, attributed in part to the introduction of the birth control pill, which first went on the market in the early 1960s.

As a result, Gen X has fewer members than the baby boomers, the Y, and the Z (born during the late 1990s and early 2000s) generations that follow it. This is one reason Generation X is often considered forgotten or overlooked in discussions about generations.

For these women (estimated at around 700,000,000 globally), the general outlook is divided. On the one hand, Gen X women face a 'sandwich generation' crisis of caring for aging parents and adult children, compounded by significant workplace ageism and discrimination, particularly after taking time off for family.

Gen X women also deal with widespread physical and mental health issues, including burnout and financial instability related to debt and inadequate retirement savings. The

Australian National Study of Mental Health and Wellbeing 2020-2022 study revealed that 21.1% of females had an anxiety disorder, and 8.6% had an affective disorder.

Additionally, these women tell me there's a pervasive issue of social invisibility and feeling overlooked by society and the job market.

The Debt Burden

Data from the global information services company Experian (which is also echoed in Australia) reveals that Gen X, along with millennials, are far more likely to have unmanageable debt than other generations.

While 27% of Gen X respondents said they have unmanageable unsecured debt, only 18% of Gen Z and 15% of baby boomers said the same. Only millennials came in higher, with 28% saying they had unsecured debt that is unmanageable.

When broken down by gender, men had a slight edge on women, with only 1 in 5 reporting unmanageable debt, compared to 1 in 4 women.

These figures are sobering, serving as a call to women approaching 50 or already in that decade to plan their future lives.

Shedding Expectations Isn't Rebellion—It's Renewal.

However, the outlook isn't all bleak, as Melissa Houston writes in a recent *Forbes Women* article, "Not Following Tradition: How Gen X Women Are Reinventing Success." She states that "Gen X women are redefining what it means to age, refusing to accept the idea that life slows down after 50."

Houston explains that women are stepping into new roles, launching businesses, and pursuing passions they may have set aside earlier in life.

"For many, the 50-plus milestone is a time to shed the expectations of others and explore their true desires," she says.

This sentiment is reflected in a report by the Australian Small Business and Family Enterprise Ombudsman (ASBFEO), revealing that in the decade leading up to 2019, two-thirds of newly established businesses were led by women. However, while 38% of all small businesses are now female-owned, there's still a gender gap to address.

ASBFEO also highlights that boosting the number of female entrepreneurs to parity with men could add between $71 billion - $135 billion to the Australian economy.

According to Dr. Sheree Gregory from Western Sydney University's School of Business, a new project is exploring factors (such as access to sponsors, mentorship, and investment funding) that may encourage diverse female entrepreneurs. She states that this could expand Australia's innovative talent pool by highlighting obstacles and tools encountered by diverse female entrepreneurs on the path to funding, creating, and growing new businesses.

Meanwhile, a staggering revelation comes from financial giant AMP in its 2025 Retirement Confidence Pulse Report. 2,000 Australians were surveyed by an independent research company, Dynata, in July 2025, and found that 50% of Australians do not feel secure about their retirement.

AMP's research also showed that women in particular have heightened insecure feelings about retirement, with only 2 in 5 women feeling confident that they will be financially stable once they stop working, as opposed to nearly 3 in 5 men.

This is not surprising, as data from the Australian Bureau of Statistics reveals that a significant proportion of women over 60 retire with an annual income less than $20,000, which is below the poverty line in Australia. Despite the labor force participation rate for women over 45 improving, women continue to face barriers such as ageism and gender bias.

Key Statistics on Australian Women's Retirement Finances

Average Superannuation Balance at Retirement (2023):	Women: $156,000 | Men: $370,000 (APRA Insights, 2023)
Super Gap for Women:	Balances ~42% of men's, largely due to career gaps and lower wages
Reliance on Age Pension:	41% of women 65+ rely partly on the pension (ABS, 2022)
Retirement Security:	Half of women 60–65 have balances under $200,000; many retire on <$20,000/year
Age Pension Dependence:	1 million Australians (mostly women 60+) depend primarily on pension income

When Marriage Meant the End of Work

Women of my mother's generation, badged the Builders, born into the Great Depression and raised through the hardship of World War II, faced insurmountable challenges when it came to pursuing professional working lives.

My mother, Angela, knew those barriers all too well. In her early 20s, armed with high results in the Leaving Certificate (precursor to the Higher School Certificate), she worked in a responsible role for a large Australian public service entity. She loved the work, was good at it, and wanted to stay.

But in 1955, when she became pregnant with me, the New South Wales Marriage Bar (1) forced her out. The rule was simple and brutal: married women and pregnant women were required to resign, their jobs reserved for men.

This policy, which existed across Australia, was only abolished in 1966. It created generations of women who were legally forced into financial dependence on their husbands, regardless of their talents or ambitions.

"The Public Service Act 1902 made the exclusion of married women legal. Five years later, the Harvester Judgment created a labor market based on the male breadwinner. Women were given low-skilled jobs with lower pay, and less job security and promotion opportunities than jobs reserved for men.

It was argued that the primary role of a married woman was to care for her family and that women were unable to manage the competing demands of domestic and paid work. Opponents of the marriage bar argued the talents and contributions of women were being wasted."

My mother was the eldest of five sisters. Each of them had their career prospects cut short. Their lives were impacted by a lack of personal financial security, while their families struggled under the added strains of raising children on a single income.

To younger women today, this may sound unthinkable. Yet, it wasn't so long ago.

Turning Points That Transformed Women's Futures

The world shifted slowly. A crucial milestone was the Sex Discrimination Act 1984 (Cth), championed by Labor Senator Susan Ryan. For the first time in Australian history, discrimination based on sex, pregnancy, marital status, or family responsibilities was made unlawful. Sexual harassment was formally recognized and outlawed. This landmark legislation changed not only workplaces but the way society saw women's rights.

Another turning point in the road to equality was the abolition of university fees in 1974. Until then, higher education was primarily the privilege of wealthy families. When the Whitlam Labor government was elected in 1972 and kept its election promise and removed fees, the gates opened for young women like me from upper working-class families in Sydney's outer western suburbs. Until then, for high female achievers, our working future was defined by secretarial college, teachers' college, or nursing.

I didn't like any of those choices.

As a result, I was accepted and enrolled in Australia's first-ever bachelor's degree in Communications. In 1978, I graduated with a Distinction in Journalism from the NSW Institute of Technology (soon to become the University of Technology, Sydney (UTS). I am the first person in my family to graduate from university.

My mother could not have been prouder. She had stood by me when my father questioned the point of higher education for a girl who would "just marry and have children."

For women like myself, my mother, and her sisters, this degree was more than an academic achievement: it was a victory against decades of systemic exclusion.

The abolition of university fees reshaped not only my future but the lives of thousands of Australian women. And by extension, it reshaped families, workplaces, and society.

Facing Old Barriers in New Forms

Of course, even with education, success wasn't straightforward.

After graduation, despite excellent grades and an article published in a national newspaper, *The Nation Review*, I struggled to secure a journalism cadetship. There were only a handful available at major newspapers and the Australian Broadcasting Commission (ABC), and although I made the short-lists, these went, as they often did, to men.

Determined to secure a job with a publishing company, I accepted a position as a production assistant at *Rydges Business Journal.* Despite regularly sub-editing the work of male editors, when I asked for a basic journalist grade, I was told bluntly by the editor: "No, women can't write about business." This was the late 1970s. It would be years before the Sex Discrimination Act forced organizations like *Rydges* to change their policies and mindsets.

Fast forward to today, and women outnumber men in higher education completions: 61% of undergraduates and 55% of postgraduates in 2022. Women aged 18-54 have consistently held higher qualifications than men since 2001.

We've come a long way—but challenges remain, particularly for women over 50 redefining success in midlife.

Exercise: Resetting Your Mindset

1. **Rewrite the Script**
   Sit quietly and write three important messages that have emerged for you from this chapter.

2. **Generational Reflection**
   Write a short reflection (one page max) on how your mother's or grandmother's career opportunities compare with yours. Notice the differences in barriers and possibilities—and then consider what barriers you may still be unconsciously carrying.

3. **Your Turning Point Story**
   Recall a moment in your life when you defied expectations and succeeded despite doubt. Capture it in a short paragraph. Keep it as a reminder: you've done it before, and you can do it again.

4. **Debt and Dreams Journal**
   If financial security weighs heavily on you, write down your current financial fears in one column, and in the next column, brainstorm one step (even a small one) that could move you toward greater stability. Sometimes naming the fear takes away its power.

✨ Key Takeaways: Success Has No Expiry Date

- **Age is not a barrier; it's an advantage.** Your experience, resilience, and networks are assets younger generations don't yet have.

- **Generational progress matters.** Understanding the barriers your mother's and grandmother's generation faced highlights how far you've come and how much further you can go.

- **Challenges persist.** Debt, ageism, and financial insecurity are real, but awareness is the first step toward action.

- **Reinvention is possible at any stage.** Gen X women, in particular, are leading in entrepreneurship and innovation.

- **Your story is your power.** Use your lived experiences as fuel for the next chapter of your career or business journey.

♀ CLAIRE'S TIP

"Remember: success after 50 isn't about chasing what society once told you to value—it's about creating a definition of success that is entirely your own. Whether that's financial independence, creative expression, or simply living with freedom, you hold the pen to write your strongest chapter yet."

2

The Silent Saboteurs

The most important lesson I have learned from the past 12 years is the imperative to plan for my future success.

Like many women, I had trusted my husband, and it had never occurred to me that he would be dishonest. However, there were warning signs.

What I refused to acknowledge at the time was my own deep resistance to change. I had experienced a very brief marriage in my mid-20s, which ended in a painful divorce. I had promised myself that I wouldn't go through that experience again.

So, instead of being honest with myself, I chose to accept my partner's promises and turn a blind eye to the red flags.

I now understand that I didn't want to experience "the constructive pain of growth" described by M. Scott Peck in his masterpiece, *The Road Less Traveled*.

While Peck's most famous line in his book is "Life is difficult", he also describes the "constructive pain of growth" as the necessary suffering involved in confronting and solving life's problems, which is essential for personal and spiritual growth.

Peck taught that rather than avoiding discomfort, people can choose to embrace problems with courage. He believes that using techniques like delaying gratification, accepting responsibility, dedicating oneself to the truth, and maintaining balance allows individuals to learn from pain and achieve a higher level of self-understanding.

I'm not someone who will willingly put my hand up for suffering. But, in hindsight, I can see that the warning signs I avoided, were an opportunity to grow. By not facing the problems at the time, I only delayed the greater pain that would eventually come.

While that change within me has been slow and many times painful, I have grown profoundly over the past decade.

There are many signs that women choose to ignore as they build their lives and careers, and at age 50, these signs can start to flash brightly.

When Winning Feels Dangerous: The Truth About Fear of Success

At first sight, fear of success doesn't sound like much of a fear. But it's very real, and it can hold you back in a big way.

Experts believe that it's probably not success itself that you fear, but the potential price of success. Sometimes, it's your own behind-the-scenes manipulations that keep tripping you up on the road to success.

Dr. Valerie Young, in her 70s, is a global thought leader on impostor syndrome and co-founder of the Impostor Syndrome Institute. She is also the author of the award-winning book, *The Secret Thoughts of Successful Women: Why Capable People Suffer from Impostor Syndrome and How to Thrive in Spite of It.*

Dr. Young says that fear of success occurs when you have an ongoing fear of succeeding, so much so that you might be inadvertently self-sabotaging.

"It's not that you think you're incapable of succeeding, but more about the fear of change that may come and whether you're up for it," Young explains. For example:

- You might get extra attention, but you're shy or introverted and uncomfortable with the spotlight.

- Public success may bring social or emotional isolation.

- Your achievement might alienate your peers.

- People might think you're bragging or self-promotional.

- You fear being knocked off the pedestal you didn't want to be on in the first place.

- Success may not be all it's cracked up to be.

- Success might change you, but not for the better.

Impostor Syndrome Doesn't Mean You're Broken—It Means You're Growing

Impostor syndrome, or the impostor phenomenon, is a psychological pattern where women doubt their achievements and have a persistent fear of being unmasked as a fraud, despite evidence of their competence and success.

People experiencing impostor syndrome may attribute their success to luck or external factors, feeling they haven't earned it and are deceiving others. This can lead to feelings of self-doubt, anxiety, burnout, and a reluctance to share ideas or accept praise.

Impostor syndrome is the quiet conviction that your success is a fluke, that you've somehow fooled others into believing you're more capable than you are. It's only a matter of time before you're 'found out.'

For many women over 50, this feeling can intensify during reinvention: new industries, new technology, or a visible role change can reawaken old doubts even as your résumé proves the opposite.

Dr. Young explains that these feelings aren't simply a lack of confidence, they're rules we unknowingly adopt about what competence 'should' look like. When we don't meet those internal rules, we decide we're frauds.

Young identifies five common "impostor rules" (or competence types). Recognizing your pattern is the first step to loosening its grip:

1. **The Perfectionist**
   Your rule: "If it isn't flawless, it doesn't count."
   Impact: You overlook solid wins, fixate on tiny gaps, and delay shipping your work.
   Reframe: Aim for excellence, not perfection. Progress shipped beats brilliance shelved.

2. **The Superwoman/Superman**
   Your rule: "If I were truly capable, I could handle everything—work, caregiving, health—without strain."
   Impact: Chronic overwork, resentment, and the belief that needing help proves inadequacy.
   Reframe: Capacity is strategic. Delegation and boundaries are leadership skills, not weaknesses.

3. **The Natural Genius**
   Your rule: "If I were really talented, this would come easily and quickly."
   Impact: New tools or roles feel threatening; learning curves trigger shame.
   Reframe: Mastery at 50+ is iterative. Time-on-task is intelligence in action.

4. **The Soloist**
    Your rule: "If I ask for help, it proves I'm not competent."
    Impact: Isolation, reinventing the wheel, and hidden burnout.
    Reframe: Collaboration is competence. Networks multiply impact.

5. **The Expert**
    Your rule: "I must know *everything* before I act."
    Impact: Endless courses and research, postponed visibility.
    Reframe: Share what you know now; teach as you learn. Authority grows in public.

For women in midlife, impostor feelings often sit on top of gendered and ageist narratives: the internalized idea that ambition is "unfeminine," that visibility invites judgment, or that learning new tech at 55 somehow "doesn't count." Add caregiving gaps or nonlinear careers, and it's easy to mistake a *context* for a *character flaw*.

It isn't.

Unlearning the Lie: Why Women Were Told That Ambition Was Unbecoming

Fear of success can also be referred to as 'success anxiety' or 'success phobia'. It's even been called 'achievemephobia.' Whatever you choose to call it, it's associated with a negative impact on overall life satisfaction.

For women, this fear is deeply shaped by cultural and generational expectations. Many of us were raised to believe that being 'too ambitious' made us unlikable or selfish.

Success, especially in male-dominated spaces, often came with whispers of arrogance or warnings that it would disrupt family life. By midlife, those messages can linger as internalized doubts: What will people think if I step into this role? Am I ready to handle the pressure? Will success cost me relationships?

Fear of success is not about lack of ability. In fact, it often surfaces in highly capable women who have every tool to thrive. The hesitation lies in the imagined consequences of achieving more, standing out, being criticized, or having to sustain performance at a higher level.

For women over 50, another layer is added: the worry that success might expose them to ageism, with others scrutinizing whether they 'still have it.'

BOX FEATURE: WHAT FEAR OF SUCCESS LOOKS LIKE

Fear of success often hides behind everyday behaviors that seem practical or harmless, (see list below), but together they limit growth and hold women back from their full potential:

- Low goals – Setting the bar deliberately low to avoid challenge.
- Procrastination – Stalling until opportunities quietly pass by.
- Perfectionism – Striving for the impossible, then using inevitable flaws as excuses not to proceed.
- Quitting too soon – Stopping just as success is within reach, often rationalized by 'good reasons.'
- Self-destructive patterns – Turning to unhealthy coping mechanisms (e.g., substance abuse) that derail progress.

These patterns create a cycle of mixed emotions. A 2001 study of athletes and performing artists found common themes of:

> - Guilt about asserting themselves too strongly in competition.
> - Anxiety about surpassing someone else's achievements.
> - Pressure to equal or surpass their own best performance, again and again.
>
> Any of these can quietly sabotage success and prevent women from fully stepping into their potential.

Exercise: Naming and Reframing Fear of Success

- **Spot the Pattern:** Read through the list of behaviors detailed in the box above (low goals, procrastination, perfectionism, quitting too soon, self-destructive habits). Circle or highlight the one(s) that feel most familiar to you.
- **Name the Fear:** For each behavior you circled, ask yourself: "What am I really afraid might happen if I succeed?" Write down your honest answers e.g., "If I succeed, people will expect too much from me," or "If I succeed, I'll outshine someone I care about."
- **Reframe the Thought:** Take each fear and rewrite it into a positive statement that empowers you. For example:
- **Fear:** "If I succeed, people will expect too much from me."

- **Reframe:** "If I succeed, it shows I'm capable, and I get to set my own boundaries."
- **Choose One Action Step:** Commit to a small action this week that moves you forward despite the fear. It could be sending an email, applying for a role, or sharing your work publicly.

Practical ways to move through it:

- **Evidence file:** Keep a simple wins log—emails of thanks, outcomes, numbers moved. When doubt spikes, review the receipts.
- **Language audit:** Replace "I was lucky" with "I prepared" or "I delivered." Name the skills you used.
- **Right-size the ask:** Ship the draft, take the call, post the update. Micro-actions build macro-confidence.
- **Peer mirrors:** Ask two trusted colleagues to reflect your strengths. Borrow their language for your bio and LinkedIn.
- **Teach once, learn twice:** Offer a short workshop or mentor hour. Teaching exposes how much you already know.

Most importantly, understand that impostor thoughts are common in high achievers, they're a sign you're stretching, not collapsing.

As Dr. Young notes, the goal isn't to *never* feel like an impostor; it's to act with courage anyway, guided by healthier rules of competence: learning is allowed, help is smart, progress counts, and your decades of experience are not an asterisk; they're your advantage.

✨ Key Takeaways: Fear of Success & Impostor Syndrome

- **Success can feel threatening, not just rewarding.** Fear of success often shows up as procrastination, perfectionism, or quitting just as progress is within reach. It's less about lack of ambition and more about fear of what success might *demand*: visibility, responsibility, or disruption of old identities.

- **Impostor syndrome thrives on "rules" of competence.** As Dr. Young notes, many women unconsciously believe success only counts if it comes easily, flawlessly, or alone. These hidden standards keep us from recognizing our real achievements.

- **Both patterns create self-sabotage.** Whether by downplaying wins, over-preparing endlessly, or withdrawing from opportunities, these fears prevent women from stepping fully into their power, especially at midlife when opportunities for reinvention are ripe.

- **Awareness is the first antidote.** Naming your pattern, whether perfectionist, natural genius, or fear of visibility, makes it easier to interrupt. Evidence logs, reframing language, and micro-actions help reclaim confidence.

- **Courage grows through action.** Both fears are overcome not by waiting for the feelings to vanish, but by moving forward in spite of them. Each step builds proof that you are capable, ready, and worthy of the opportunities you're pursuing.

♀ CLAIRE'S TIP

"I've learned that the very moments when I felt most like a fraud, or most scared of what success might bring, were usually signs I was on the verge of real growth. Instead of retreating, I began to treat those feelings as invitations: to step forward, to claim my space, to prove to myself what I already knew deep down. If you feel the fear or the doubt, don't stop; that's your compass pointing to where your next breakthrough lies."

3

The Old Vision Wasn't Designed for You.

Most women at 30 were defining success by a template created by men and for men: climbing the corporate ladder, earning promotions, or keeping up with peers on the expected timeline: house, children, senior role, financial milestones. By 50, those definitions often feel narrow, outdated, and unsatisfying.

At this stage, success is less about external approval and more about alignment with who you truly are. It's about asking: What matters to me now? How do I want to live, work, and contribute in the years ahead? How do I define prosperity, fulfillment, and freedom?

For many women, success becomes more holistic:

Financial security: Creating a platform that supports choice and independence.
Fulfillment: Doing meaningful work that lights you up.
Freedom: Choosing when, how, and with whom you work.
Authenticity: Living and working in alignment with your values and passions.

It's challenging to pursue fulfillment or freedom without financial security. Gen X women and those now in their 50s and early 60s face significant burdens already highlighted:

- Higher mortgage debt into retirement.
- Rising cost-of-living pressures.
- Later entry into serious financial planning.

- Sandwich responsibilities, career peak demands, while supporting both children and aging parents.

Many carry substantial debt, and some face renting or downsizing in retirement. US author Ada Calhoun describes this starkly in her book *Why We Can't Sleep: Women's New Midlife Crisis*:

"Gen X women who feel like they have been given the world are crushed by the burden of having to carry it, and are ashamed by the sense of failure when they inevitably can't."

Her words resonate globally. For many of us, success now must include financial resilience. It's not about wealth for wealth's sake; it's about money as a foundation for freedom, sanity, and choice.

"If you were a middle-class girl born in the U.S. between 1965 and 1980—typically defined as Generation X—you might have grown up thinking you had it made. Thanks to Title IX, [comprehensive federal rights law in the United States that prohibits sex-based discrimination in any education program or activity receiving federal funding], you could excel at sports on the field of your choice; thanks to boomer women who banged down doors in the workplace, you could excel at a job in the field of your choice.

"And you could be a mom, too—because you'd be married to a proudly evolved guy who knew his way around a dirty diaper. You were among the first generation of women for whom 'having it all' wasn't a ludicrous fantasy," Calhoun states.

Calhoun's book was reviewed by Corrie Pikul at Oprah.com, which proclaimed, *"Why We Can't Sleep Is the Midlife Crisis Book Every Woman Needs to Read After 40."*

On reading this, Connie Pikul comments that, "Most of those Gen X girls are now women in their 40s and 50s. And for many, things haven't turned out as they'd hoped. Yes, they may have careers and kids, but a sense of fulfillment eludes them.

"Three years ago, after she published a wry, sometimes rueful ode to marriage—an acquaintance called and said, "I just read your book, and I think you're having a midlife crisis," Calhoun said she was sceptical.

"Her? Crisis? And yet she identified with all the free-floating malaise that had become a constant in conversations she'd been having with women her age," Pikul writes.

In her book, Calhoun claims that many of these women were raised to believe they would live the dreams their mothers and grandmothers couldn't. "For example, a girl might say she wanted to be a nurse, and her mom would counter with, "Why not a doctor?"

"This was well-intentioned, but it created a steady pressure for us to achieve more while continuing to manage the caregiving and housekeeping responsibilities that, as it turned out, continued to fall largely to women.

"So we get to midlife, the time when we're supposed to be at the top of our game, and it's a bit of a shock: Women talked about not having the family they wanted or the career they imagined or the money they expected. I can't count how many women looked at me and said, "What did I do wrong?" Calhoun adds.

The Life You Crave Must Have Three Ingredients: Fulfillment, Freedom, and Truth

Calhoun talked to more than 200 Gen X women from across the U.S., of different religious, ethnic, cultural, and political backgrounds. All were middle-class. When asked why, she explains:

"I was intrigued by women who, by virtue of class, grew up with reasonable expectations of opportunity, success, and fulfillment, yet are still floundering. Poor women in this country struggle under burdens that are beyond the scope of this discussion, while the very rich—well, *The Real Housewives* has them covered. I wanted to talk about the vast middle, the women like me who think of themselves as lucky, and who by any measure are lucky, yet are deeply frustrated."

If we take Calhoun's research to be true, then we are facing more than a midlife crisis. I believe that globally we are in the midst of an existential crisis: a period of deep questioning and reflection on the meaning of life, one's purpose, and the nature of existence. It's a state that can often lead to feelings of anxiety, despair, or confusion.

These profound thoughts may arise from major life transitions or significant losses, prompting a search for deeper meaning, a more authentic self, and a sense of purpose in a potentially meaningless world.

I write from experience.

Once I accepted that I had to close my business, I went into survival mode, mostly guided by my compassionate accountant, Warwick Hill from Trood Pratt in Sydney. He organized meetings with the ATO and sat with me while we explained to them why we couldn't continue to pay the debt I had inherited.

They agreed to absolve the debt, and then they took any assets remaining, including my laptop, which they allowed me to buy back for $100.

I went to bed and didn't come out for two weeks. To say it was an existential crisis was an understatement. I thought my life was over. My rational mind couldn't understand or process how this had happened. I keep thinking that if only I could wake up, the nightmare would be over.

My energy reserves were minimal, but I had enough to walk around the block to a yoga center and eventually began to take classes. Pursuing my previously highly charged life, I had no time for yoga because, obviously, it would slow me down. Now I had plenty of time.

Once I took my first steps back into a world, now very different from the one I had left, my recipe for healing came organically:

- **Accept the crisis:**
  View it as a normal and potentially positive turning point for self-reflection, rather than something to fight.

- **Embrace uncertainty:**
  Recognize that a lack of answers is a part of life and can be a path to finding personal meaning.

- **Sit with your feelings:**
  Take time to understand your emotions instead of trying to suppress them, which can lead to deeper self-discovery.

- **Connect with loved ones:**
  Share your feelings and experiences to combat feelings of isolation and receive external perspectives.

- **Talk to professionals:**
  A therapist can help you assess your values, find meaning, and work through difficult thoughts and emotions.

- **Explore values:**
  Re-evaluate your core values and commit to goals that align with the person you want to be.

- **Engage with spirituality or philosophy:**
  Explore existing belief systems or philosophical frameworks for answers to life's big questions.

- **Practice gratitude:**
  Keep a gratitude journal or prioritize activities that bring joy to shift your perspective and appreciate the present.

- **Create meaning through commitment:**
  Choose to live ethically and make meaningful commitments to people, projects, or ideals.

I started to understand that beyond finances, success at this stage for me meant fulfillment in all areas of my life, including waking up excited about work, knowing it matters, and seeing the impact I create.

For women that Ada Calhoun describes, it means using decades of skills and wisdom in ways that energize, not drain.

It also means freedom: the ability to design work around your life rather than the other way around. Freedom to say yes to energizing projects and no to obligations that deplete you.

Finally, this new success is about authenticity and courage: embracing your unique perspective, taking calculated risks, learning new skills, and living life on your own terms.

Exercise: Define Your Success

Reflect on the Past. What did "success" mean to you at 30? Promotions, titles, approval?

- **Notice the Shift.** What matters most now? Health, family, freedom, creativity?

- **Visualize Your Ideal Life.** Picture your life in 1–5 years. What work do you do? What relationships do you nurture? What freedoms do you enjoy?

- **Write Your Definition.** Create a success statement: 'Success means doing work I love, earning enough to live freely, and having time to travel and grow personally.'

- **Align with Action.** List 2–3 small steps to bring your life closer to that vision.

- **Daily Reminder.** Place your success statement somewhere visible. Revisit it every morning.

Values, Passions, and Lifestyle Alignment—The Trifecta of Your Meaningful Next Act

Midlife brings clarity. You now know what drains you and what energizes you. Success is not about keeping up; it's about aligning work with your deepest values and passions.

Too many women have found themselves out of alignment: pursuing paths that once made sense but now feel hollow. This misalignment can cause burnout or a nagging sense that something is missing.

The good news? You now have the wisdom, skills, and perspective to recalibrate. Alignment is not just a dream. It's a strategy.

Success, Re-written: How These Women Turned the Rules Upside Down

Leanne, 52 – From Corporate Climb to Inner Calm

After 25 years in corporate HR, Leanne had the title, the salary, the corner office—and constant burnout. She realized she was chasing a version of success that no longer fit who she was becoming. So, she left.

Today, she runs her own wellness coaching practice, helping other women reconnect with their bodies and purpose. She earns less than she did before, but lives more. Her days are filled with meaning, movement, and freedom. As she puts it, "I finally feel like I'm working *with* my life, not against it."

Maya, 57 – Reinventing Work on Her Own Terms

Teaching was once her passion, but after decades in the system, Maya felt boxed in and burnt out. She made a bold pivot: retrained in digital marketing, took a few freelance gigs, and eventually built a thriving consultancy.

Now she helps mission-driven non-profits grow their reach online. She earns more than she did in the classroom and chooses exactly who she works with. "I didn't just change careers," she says. "I reclaimed my power."

Jennifer, 61 – From Finance to Fulfillment

Jennifer spent most of her career in high-stakes finance, managing portfolios and pressure. But as she neared her 60s, her priorities shifted. She stepped away from the boardroom and stepped into service—joining two non-profit boards and mentoring young women entering the workforce.

There's no six-figure bonus attached, but the impact is priceless. "I've had money," she says. "Now I want meaning."

Each woman proves: success after 50 is not a one-size-fits-all definition. It's a personal vision.

✨ Key Takeaways: Clarify Your Vision

- Success at 50+ is not what it was at 30—it's richer, more personal, and more aligned.

- Financial security provides the foundation for freedom and fulfillment.

- Fulfillment means doing work that matters; freedom means designing life on your terms.

- Authenticity and courage are the hallmarks of success in midlife.

- Alignment of values, passions, and lifestyle is the strategy for thriving.

💡 CLAIRE'S TIP

"Success is not a destination; it's a definition, and you get to write it. Don't borrow someone else's version. Each morning, ask yourself:
'Am I living in alignment with what matters most to me?'
If the answer is no, take one small step today to close that gap. Over time, those small steps create a life that feels not only successful but truly yours."

4

Transferable Talents: Your New Passport

It took decades for me to accumulate the skills, wisdom, and insights that I carry today. Some were earned formally, through qualifications, job titles, or promotions. Others came quietly, shaped by family responsibilities, volunteer work, or simply living through the highs and lows of life.

You already possess an extraordinary set of transferable skills, but like many women over 50, you may not always recognize their value or give yourself credit.

This chapter is about pressing pause to take stock. When you know what you bring to the table, you can walk into new opportunities with clarity and confidence. When you can articulate your strengths to others, whether in a CV, interview, boardroom, or even a café conversation, doors begin to open.

The Power of Taking Stock

Paradoxically, the first step in moving forward is to look back. This isn't about dwelling on the past but about noticing patterns, talents, and triumphs that can shape your future.

When you list the roles you've held, professional, personal, and community, you start to see the sheer breadth of your contributions. Perhaps you've coordinated a school fundraiser, managed workplace teams, learned new technology, mentored colleagues, or cared for family.

Each of these experiences represents skills in action—leadership, organization, adaptability, and resilience. Yet women often dismiss them as "just what I had to do."

Margaret, 62 – From Teacher to Corporate Trainer

Margaret had been a high school English teacher for nearly 30 years. When she retired early, she felt unsure of what to do next. But as she listed her achievements, she realized she had designed lesson plans, delivered presentations daily, managed classrooms, and mentored younger teachers. These are competencies sought in corporate learning. With reframing, she became a sought-after trainer.

Taking stock is more than listing skills. It's about identifying patterns—the threads that connect your happiest, most energizing moments. Ask: What work energizes you? What achievements bring a smile? What have others consistently praised you for? Patterns reveal both competence and preference.

Amina, 55 – The Volunteer Who Found Her Business Mojo

Amina spent years volunteering at a local refugee center, organizing and mentoring. She thought of it as "just helping out." Later, she saw her pattern: she thrived when empowering women. This became the seed of her consultancy helping migrant women start businesses.

Every achievement holds transferable assets—leadership, empathy, financial management, creativity. The key is articulating them in professional language that resonates with employers or clients.

Janine, 70 – Board Director at Last

Janine had been a nurse for 40 years. She thought she was "*just a nurse.*" In fact, she had supervised teams, managed budgets, advocated for patients, and trained juniors. Within a year, she joined two health boards. At 70, she shaped policy with lived experience as authority.

Cut Down to Size: The Silent Cost of Standing Tall

When Julie received the news of her promotion to senior partner, she expected congratulations. Instead, her success was met with silence, even whispers of "she's gotten too big for her boots." What should have been a moment of celebration left her shrinking back, questioning whether she had made a mistake by daring to rise.

This is the quiet cruelty of the Tall Poppy Syndrome, where women who dare to stand tall are often cut down, not by strangers, but by colleagues, friends, and even peers. It's a cultural reflex that punishes ambition and makes women second-guess the very success they've worked so hard to achieve.

The Tall Poppy Syndrome remains alive and well in Australia, and it's reasonable to say that older women are discouraged from "blowing their own trumpet." I have consistently coached women who struggled to identify and promote their own achievements.

Now that I don't work in an office, I have my university degree framed and mounted on a wall in my home. I have business cards that state I'm an author and coach, and I regularly update my business social media branding.

These are your intellectual assets; they have been hard-earned by this stage of your life, and each of these achievements is more than a memory—it's a launchpad for your next opportunity. The key is learning to translate what you've done into what you *can do* next.

Although this may be challenging, start by identifying your standout achievements. What successes make you smile when you think of them?

Don't just focus on outcomes, look at the skills, strategies, and resilience that made them possible. These are transferable assets, ready to be applied in new contexts.

For example, leading a team through a challenging project demonstrates leadership, communication, and problem-solving skills valuable in consulting, mentoring, or even starting your own business.

Next, consider how your experience intersects with current opportunities. Where could your unique combination of skills, insights, and networks meet a need in the market or workplace? By framing your past achievements as evidence of capability, you create confidence and credibility with yourself and others.

Finally, take action. Identify one or two opportunities that excite you and map how your experience makes you uniquely qualified. Treat each step as a bridge between what you've accomplished and what you want to achieve next.

Your past is not a limitation—it's a toolkit for reinvention.

The Circle That Lifts You Higher

One of the biggest lessons many women learn after 50 is that you can't do it all alone—nor should we try. For decades, you may have been the one holding everything together:

raising children, supporting partners, managing careers, and caring for parents. But now, in this stage of reinvention, it's your turn to be supported. Building a support circle is not a luxury; it's a lifeline.

A strong support circle provides emotional, practical, and professional strength. It reminds you that you're not alone, even when challenges feel overwhelming. For many women, midlife can feel isolating: adult children have left home, work identities may be shifting, and friendships built around school runs or younger years may have faded. That's why deliberately creating a circle of people who uplift and encourage you is so important.

Your support circle doesn't need to be large; in fact, depth matters more than breadth. Think of it as a small but powerful ecosystem:

- **Mentors and role models** who have navigated similar transitions and can offer wisdom.
- **Peers** who are walking the same journey and can relate to your experiences in real time.
- **Younger voices** who bring fresh perspectives, digital know-how, and a sense of vitality.
- **Trusted professionals** such as coaches, health practitioners, or financial advisors who can help you make informed decisions.

Together, this circle becomes a mirror reflecting your strengths back to you when you forget them. They also become your sounding board for new ideas and your safety net in times of difficulty.

Anne, 56 – Confidence Builder

Anne launched her consulting business at 56. At first, she worked quietly and alone, but progress was slow, and self-doubt crept in. When she intentionally built a support circle by joining a women's entrepreneur network, reconnecting with an old mentor, and leaning on her closest friends for encouragement, her confidence shifted.

Within two years, she had grown her business, published thought leadership articles, and was mentoring others. Her support circle didn't just cheer her on; they helped her see possibilities she couldn't see for herself.

Equally, support circles protect against burnout. Women are often conditioned to keep giving until they're empty, but a healthy circle encourages reciprocity. Sometimes you will be the one offering advice or comfort, and at other times you'll be the one receiving it. That ebb and flow builds resilience.

If you don't yet have a strong circle, start small. Reach out to two or three people you already trust. Join a group that excites you, such as a professional association, book club, or online community. Over time, your circle will grow naturally, shaped by shared values and mutual respect.

Above all, remember this: you deserve a circle that nourishes you. In your second act, surrounding yourself with the right people is not just about connection, it's about creating the conditions where you can thrive, flourish, and step boldly into the future.

Take five minutes to jot down the names of five people who could form the foundation of your support circle. Reach out to one of them this week. A coffee, a call, or even a simple note of appreciation can begin weaving your circle stronger.

Action: The Magic Step

If you are not taking action, then it's likely that you will be living in a fantasy where dreams dominate. Courage is not something we wait for; it's something we build. And the way we build it is through action, one small, deliberate step at a time.

For women over 50, courage often means daring to step outside long-established roles, routines, and expectations. It can feel intimidating to launch a new business, apply for a fresh role, or simply say "yes" to opportunities that once felt too bold. But here's the truth: courage doesn't grow in the abstract. It expands each time you act, even in the face of uncertainty.

Think of courage like a muscle. If it's never exercised, it weakens. But every time you use it, making the call, raising your hand, applying for that board position, you strengthen it. The beauty of being over 50 is that you've already demonstrated courage countless times: in raising families, navigating challenges, rebuilding after setbacks, or persevering through health or financial struggles.

You already have proof that you can be brave. Now, the goal is to channel that same courage into action, shaping the future you want.

Janet, 62 – Courage Equals Opportunities

Janet, 62, had always dreamed of writing but never shared her work publicly. Then, she posted her first short essay online. She feared silence or criticism. Instead, her inbox filled with messages from women who said her words gave them strength. That single act of courage pressing 'publish' created a ripple effect that expanded her confidence and opened doors to speaking opportunities she never imagined.

Courage is contagious. When you take a bold step, others notice. You model possibilities for friends, colleagues, even family members. Often, women underestimate the influence they have simply by daring to try. Your courage doesn't just move you forward; it gives others permission to step forward too.

Of course, action doesn't always mean grand gestures. Sometimes the bravest thing is something small: asking a question in a meeting, updating your LinkedIn profile to reflect your new direction, or attending an event alone. These micro-acts of courage stack up over time, creating momentum. And momentum is what transforms fear into confidence.

One powerful way to expand courage is to reframe fear itself. Instead of asking, "What if I fail?", try asking, "What if this works?" That subtle shift opens up space for possibility. It changes action from something risky into something filled with potential.

Another key is accountability. Share your goal with someone in your support circle and ask them to check in with you. Courage grows when we know we're not alone in our efforts.

Above all, remember: courage isn't about being fearless. It's about moving forward *despite* the fear. Every action you take proves to yourself that you are capable, resilient, and ready for what's next.

Identify one small action you've been avoiding because of fear. Write it down and commit to doing it within the next week. When you complete it, take a moment to celebrate, because with every step, you're expanding your courage and unlocking new possibilities.

Age: The One Superpower You Earn

For so long, women have been told that age is something to hide, deny, or battle against. Wrinkles must be smoothed away, grey hair dyed, birthdays whispered about. But what if we flipped that script entirely? What if age wasn't a burden to be managed but a superpower to be wielded?

By the time you reach 50, 60, or 70, you have lived through enough triumphs and setbacks to know what really matters. That kind of clarity is priceless. Younger professionals may have energy and fresh ideas, but you bring perspective—the ability to see the long game, to cut through distractions, and to act with wisdom. That isn't a liability; it's a strength.

Vivienne Westwood, 81 – Disrupter to The End

Consider women like UK fashion designer Vivienne Westwood, who was still disrupting the industry into her 80s, writing regularly on issues of climate and social justice on her website *No Man's Land*.

Her age wasn't a hindrance; it was the very thing that gave her work depth, authenticity, and resonance. She wasn't competing with twenty-somethings; she was creating from a lifetime of experiences, turning age into an edge.

One of the superpowers of age is resilience. By now, you've already survived storms, financial upheavals, health challenges, family crises, or professional setbacks. Each one has made you tougher, wiser, and more adaptable. While others may fear failure, you know it's not the end; it's often the beginning of something new. That calm in the storm, that refusal to be shaken, is the mark of true leadership.

Another gift of age is confidence. Many women in midlife talk about the liberation that comes with caring less about what others think. You've already proven yourself, carried responsibilities, and overcome doubts. There is a lightness that comes with no longer needing external validation. This freedom fuels boldness, whether that's speaking up in boardrooms, starting a new business, or finally pursuing a long-held creative dream.

And then there is empathy. Years of walking through different stages of life, of supporting friends, partners, children, and colleagues, have expanded your capacity to understand people. In workplaces and communities, this emotional intelligence is invaluable. It creates teams that thrive, relationships that last, and decisions that consider more than just short-term wins.

The world often equates financial value with youth and speed, but longevity teaches something different: endurance. Superpowers aren't always about moving fast, they're about knowing when to move, when to pause, and how to keep going for the long run. That's why so many women in their later years find themselves excelling in leadership, mentoring, and creative work. Age sharpens the qualities that matter most.

So instead of apologizing for your age, claim it. Every year you've lived is fuel for your wisdom, resilience, empathy, and courage. Age doesn't diminish your power; it multiplies it. And when you show up with the confidence to see age as your greatest asset, you give permission for other women and younger generations to embrace theirs, too.

Your age is not your weakness. It's your superpower. Use it boldly.

The Bigger Picture: Why This Matters

When talking about career reinvention, building new skills, or finding the courage to start again after 50, it's easy to focus only on the personal benefits: greater confidence, financial security, or fulfillment. These are vital outcomes, but the bigger picture is even more powerful.

Every woman who chooses to step forward at this stage of life is doing more than transforming her own future; she is reshaping society's understanding of what it means to age, to work, and to thrive.

For decades, the narrative has been that women's prime years belong to youth. Advertisements, workplaces, and even cultural traditions have often sidelined women past a certain age, suggesting invisibility or irrelevance. Yet when women over 50 reclaim their voice, their creativity, and their professional presence, they disrupt that outdated story.

They remind everyone, employers, communities, and younger generations, that value, wisdom, and ambition do not have an expiry date.

This matters for future generations, too. A granddaughter who sees her grandmother start a business at 65 or publish a book at 70 learns that life's possibilities don't close with age, they expand. A daughter who watches her mother pivot into a new career after 50 understands that resilience and reinvention are lifelong skills. By showing up boldly, you leave a living legacy that echoes far beyond your own life.

On a societal level, the stakes are high. Women over 50 are the fastest-growing segment of the workforce in many countries. Their participation is not just a matter of personal fulfillment but an economic necessity. When experienced women withdraw because of bias, lack of support, or self-doubt, industries lose vital talent and perspective. Conversely, when they remain active, engaged, and innovative, entire economies benefit.

As Dr. Sheree Gregory has stated, in Australia alone, closing the gender participation gap in the workforce could add billions to the country's GDP each year.

There is also the matter of representation. Boards, governments, and businesses that include women over 50 gain access to decision-making shaped by decades of lived experience. This leads to more balanced policies, more inclusive practices, and more humane workplaces. It is no coincidence that organizations with diverse leadership consistently outperform those without it.

The bigger picture is also about social change and mitigating the sense of a looming existential crisis.

When women over 50 claim visibility, they challenge stereotypes not only about gender but about aging itself. They push back against the notion that life slows down, insisting instead that it can accelerate into its most meaningful chapter. They create cultural permission for everyone, men and women alike, to imagine vibrant, purposeful later years.

Ultimately, this matters because it's about freedom. The freedom to define success on your own terms. The freedom to step away from limitations, whether imposed by society or internalized through years of doubt. And the freedom to build a life that reflects your true values, passions, and ambitions.

Your second act isn't just about you. It's part of a much larger movement, one that is rewriting the script for what's possible after 50. Every bold choice you make becomes part of a collective voice saying: *"We are here. We are capable. And our strongest years are still ahead."*

Careers That Fit Your Life, Not the Other Way Around

I have often felt that the thought of stepping into a 'second act' was too daunting and overwhelming. I would try to persuade myself to have a smaller life: shopping, friends, and Netflix.

It has never worked.

During my training as a coach, I learned that commitment is a curious thing. According to Johann Wolfgang Von Goethe:

"Until one is committed, there is always hesitancy, the chance to draw back, always ineffectiveness. Concerning all acts of initiative and creation, there is one elementary truth, the ignorance of which kills countless ideas and splendid plans: that the moment one definitely commits oneself, then providence moves too.

All sorts of things occur to help one that would never otherwise have occurred. A whole stream of events issues from the decision, raising to one's favor all manner of unforeseen incidents, meetings, and material assistance which no one could have dreamed would come her way. Whatever you can do or dream, you can begin it. Boldness has genius, power, and magic in it."

Goethe who passed in 1832, was German and a polymath widely regarded as the most influential writer in the German language. His work has had a wide-ranging influence on literary, and philosophical thought to the present day.

He says, once the decision is made to commit to change, the next steps seem to materialize.

The question now isn't, "Where to start?" It has evolved into "What now?"

What defines this stage of life isn't limitations, it's about liberation. It's an opportunity to design a career that truly reflects your values, energy, and aspirations.

Full-Time Roles

For many women over 50, a full-time role remains the most appealing option. It offers stability, structure, and often benefits such as superannuation contributions, paid leave, and healthcare. After decades of juggling work, family, and caregiving responsibilities, some women find comfort in knowing exactly when and how they will work each week. Full-time positions can also provide a sense of identity, belonging, and purpose—particularly if they are aligned with personal values and professional expertise.

However, what makes full-time work at this stage different from earlier in life is the mindset shift. Women in their 50s and 60s are not looking for a job just to climb the corporate ladder or prove themselves. Instead, they often seek roles where they can apply their hard-earned skills while working in an environment that respects balance and maturity. It's less about endless ambition and more about meaningful contribution.

Some women decide to return to a full-time role after years of part-time work or entrepreneurship, appreciating the consistency of income and the sense of structure it brings. Others remain in senior-level positions, continuing to influence and mentor within their fields. The key is that the decision is intentional, not default—chosen because it fits their life stage, values, and financial needs.

Jennifer, 62: Steady Leadership

Jennifer, 62, had spent much of her career in marketing before taking a step back in her 50s to care for her elderly parents. After several years of part-time consulting, she realized she missed the collaborative buzz of a full office environment. When an opportunity arose to join a mid-sized not-for-profit as a Communications Director, she took the leap.

What she found surprised her. Rather than feeling out of place, she became the 'anchor' of the team—mentoring younger staff, providing steady leadership, and contributing big-picture thinking drawn from decades of experience. Jennifer's role provided her with a renewed sense of purpose, financial security, and a daily rhythm that supported her well-being.

Her story is a reminder that full-time work in your 60s doesn't have to be draining or out of reach. With the right fit, it can be energizing, stabilizing, and deeply fulfilling.

Part-Time Roles

Part-time work offers one of the most balanced and flexible options for women over 50. It allows you to remain active in the workforce, maintain a sense of professional identity, and generate income—while also creating more space for personal priorities such as health, family, travel, or passion projects.

At this stage in life, many women no longer want the all-consuming demands of a 40–50-hour work week, but they also don't want to step away entirely. Part-time roles provide a middle path, where contribution and freedom can exist side by side.

One of the biggest advantages of part-time work is the ability to tailor your schedule to your energy and goals. Some women choose 2 or 3 full working days, leaving the rest of the week free. Others prefer shorter daily shifts to maintain a consistent rhythm.

Employers are increasingly recognizing the value of experienced part-time staff, especially in industries like healthcare, education, finance, and consulting, where knowledge and stability matter as much as hours clocked.

Another benefit of part-time work is the chance to explore other opportunities. A woman may choose part-time employment to keep her skills sharp and her finances steady, while also exploring creative pursuits, side hustles, or volunteering. This makes part-time work an ideal stepping stone to a portfolio career or a gradual transition into retirement.

Aisha, 57: Negotiating Freedom

Aisha, 57, had worked in finance for over 25 years. When her children grew up and left home, she realized she wanted more time for travel and creative writing, but she wasn't ready to stop working. She negotiated with her employer to shift her senior analyst role to 3 days per week.

The change gave her the freedom to spend 2 days focused on her passion for writing while still maintaining a steady income and contributing to her team. Interestingly, her productivity increased because she was more focused and energized during her workdays.

Consulting

Consulting within your area of proficiency is one of the most natural transitions for women over 50. After decades of professional experience, you carry a wealth of insights, problem-solving ability, and sector knowledge that organizations actively need. Yet many women underestimate the value of this expertise.

Consulting enables you to 'package' your skills into services that can be delivered on your own terms—project by project, client by client—without the constraints of a full-time role.

The beauty of consulting is flexibility. You choose the type of work you take on, the industries you engage with, and often, the hours you work. Some women prefer short, high-intensity projects where they can make an impact quickly and move on. Others enjoy longer advisory roles, helping an organization shape strategy, develop leadership, or manage change over time.

With consulting, there is a higher earning potential than traditional employment, since clients pay for specialized expertise and focused outcomes rather than hours alone. For women at midlife, this can be an empowering way to increase financial independence while working smarter, not harder.

Consulting is also a confidence booster. It requires you to stand firmly in the value of your skills and to present yourself as an expert. Many women find this process transformative—it helps them reframe years of "just doing the work" into a recognized professional identity that commands respect.

Maria, 62: Starting Small

Maria had spent most of her career as a senior HR manager in the corporate sector. When her company downsized, she wasn't ready to retire, but also didn't want another demanding full-time role. Instead, she began offering consulting services to smaller businesses that lacked in-house HR expertise.

She started with one client, supporting their recruitment process and advising on workplace culture. Within six months, word-of-mouth referrals brought her three more clients. Today, Maria works about 20 hours a week, setting her own schedule, while earning as much as she did in her corporate role. She says consulting has given her "a new sense of freedom" and a chance to apply her experience in more meaningful, hands-on ways.

Entrepreneurship

For women over 50, entrepreneurship is more than just starting a business—it's about taking ownership of your time, your talents, and your future. It offers the ultimate freedom: to build something aligned with your passions, values, and lifestyle. Whether it's a small side hustle, a consultancy, or a fully-fledged company, entrepreneurship can transform both your career and your confidence.

One of the biggest advantages women over 50 bring to entrepreneurship is perspective. You know how to assess risks, manage people, and navigate challenges—skills honed through decades of professional and personal experience. Unlike younger entrepreneurs, you're not starting from scratch. You already have networks, wisdom, and credibility to draw on.

Entrepreneurship also provides creative freedom. You decide what services or products to offer, how to deliver them, and who your customers will be. This autonomy is incredibly empowering, particularly if you've spent years working within rigid corporate structures or balancing other people's priorities.

For many women, launching a business is less about financial necessity and more about finally giving themselves permission to pursue something they truly care about.

It doesn't have to be high-risk either. Many women start small—testing an idea as a side hustle, experimenting with online sales, or offering services on a freelance basis. This phased approach allows you to build confidence and learn as you go without overextending financially. Over time, what begins as a modest venture can grow into something substantial, even legacy-making.

Asha, 55: Regaining Her Voice

At 55, Asha left her long career in teaching to explore a long-held passion for food and culture. She launched a small catering business from her kitchen, specializing in heritage recipes passed down from her grandmother. Initially, she catered only for friends and community events. But her unique offering quickly gained traction, and within three years, she had a thriving boutique catering company with a loyal client base.

For Asha, entrepreneurship has been about far more than income. "It gave me back my voice," she says. "I get to share my heritage, be creative every day, and earn an income doing something that feels deeply personal." Her business is now a family affair, with her daughter managing the marketing and her husband handling logistics—turning her second act into a shared legacy.

Portfolio Careers

For many women over 50, the idea of committing to just one role feels limiting. By this stage of life, you may have a diverse skill set, a wide network, and multiple passions you want to explore. A portfolio career, blending several income streams and roles—offers flexibility, variety, and resilience. Instead of being tied to a single job description, you create a professional mosaic that reflects your interests and strengths.

Portfolio careers can combine consulting, part-time employment, freelance projects, teaching, or creative ventures. For example, you might spend three days a week consulting in your field, another day coaching clients, and another pursuing a creative side business. This approach not only spreads financial risk but also keeps your work life dynamic and engaging.

The beauty of portfolio careers is that they allow you to align your professional life with your personal rhythm. If you want more time for caregiving, travel, or health, you can adjust your commitments accordingly. To scale up your income, consider adding new projects or services. It's a flexible model that adapts as your priorities change.

Another advantage is sustainability. When one stream slows down, another often picks up, creating stability across changing markets. Many women also find that portfolio careers reduce burnout—by engaging in different kinds of work, they stay stimulated, curious, and energized.

Margaret, 62: Creating Perfect Balance

Margaret decided she no longer wanted the intensity of her corporate HR director role, but she wasn't ready to stop working altogether. Instead, she built a portfolio career: 2 days a week, she consults for a non-profit organization, offering HR strategy and training. She also teaches a short university course each semester and runs a small career-coaching practice from home.

Margaret describes her week as "a perfect balance of income, freedom, and fulfillment." She enjoys the variety, the independence, and the ability to choose work that aligns with her values. Most importantly, she has control over her schedule, allowing her to care for her elderly mother and spend more time with her grandchildren.

Her portfolio career isn't just a way of working—it's a lifestyle that gives her freedom, purpose, and joy.

The New Pioneers: Women 50+ Are Quietly Taking Over the Future

- Technology: Maria, 55, retrained in UX design after a career in teaching. She now designs accessible digital platforms for education, blending her teaching knowledge with new technical skills.

- Wellness: Linda, 63, became a certified health coach after leaving corporate sales. She built an online coaching practice specializing in supporting midlife women through lifestyle transitions.

- Sustainability: Anne, 58, previously an accountant, moved into renewable energy auditing. Her financial expertise translated into helping small businesses adopt greener practices while tracking savings.

Exercise: Exploring Emerging Industries and Flexible Work

- Identify areas that energize you, or you've always wanted to explore.

- Match Skills to Industries – For each interest, write down skills or experience you could bring. Include both technical and soft skills.

- Research Emerging Industries – Look at industries experiencing growth or innovation (examples: digital marketing, wellness, sustainability, tech consulting, online education). Note which ones intersect with your interests and skills.

- Explore Flexible Work Models – Consider how you'd like to work: full-time, part-time, consulting, freelancing, portfolio careers, or remote roles. Which models best fit your lifestyle goals?

- Shortlist Opportunities – Identify 2–3 potential career paths or projects where your skills, interests, and flexibility align.

- First Action Step – Choose one opportunity and write a concrete next step to explore it (e.g., connect with a mentor, take an online course, or research companies in that field).

⭐ Key Takeaways: Exploring Career Options Over 50

- **Full-time roles** can offer structure, stability, and financial security — but only if they fit your current lifestyle and values.

- **Part-time work** provides balance and breathing room, allowing you to stay engaged while enjoying more personal freedom.

- **Consulting** allows you to package your expertise into high-impact, flexible projects, often on your own terms.

- **Entrepreneurship and side hustles** unlock creative control and independence, whether small-scale or a bold new venture.

- **Portfolio careers** weave together multiple streams of work, combining security, creativity, and adaptability into a fulfilling mosaic.

- **Emerging industries and flexible models—** from digital transformation to sustainability—are wide open to women over 50 who bring wisdom, adaptability, and life perspective.

- The secret is **clarity**: when you know your values, lifestyle needs, and passions, it's easier to choose the path (or blend of paths) that's right for you.

♀ CLAIRE'S TIP

"At this stage of life, exploring career options isn't about chasing every possibility; it's about aligning your choices with who you are now. Be open, be curious, and trust that the experience you've gained is a powerful compass. The career you step into after 50 doesn't need to look like anyone else's; it only needs to feel right for you."

5

From Gaps to Gateways: Turning Skills into Second-Act Power

When I eventually began to recover from the trauma of loss and looked at my CV, I wondered if the world had passed me by.

I see now that it was an irrational thought, but nevertheless, it was there.

Technology shifts, industries evolve and job descriptions bristle with tools and jargon that didn't exist when you first built your career. It's easy to feel left behind, but what looks like a 'gap' is really a gateway. Upskilling and reskilling aren't about starting over; they're about adding layers of power to the strengths you already carry.

Think of it this way: every new skill you acquire becomes a bridge between your deep experience and today's opportunities. Whether it's mastering a digital tool, learning leadership frameworks, or exploring an emerging industry, reskilling signals to the world and to yourself that you are adaptable, curious, and future-ready.

Often, it's challenging for women to realize that their time and energy are precious. If you're considering further training, the key is to choose learning that truly matters, training that aligns with your goals, values, and the lifestyle you want now.

This stage of life isn't about learning for the sake of it; it's about investing in skills that open doors, increase confidence, and create meaningful opportunities.

By undertaking the *'Exploring emerging industries and flexible work exercise'* in the previous chapter, you will have awakened to more career possibilities within the workplace.

Now it is time to start clarifying your Why.

The Paradigm of WHY: Unlocking Purpose, Power, and Clarity

The paradigm of WHY was made popular by the eternal optimist and author Simon Sinek in his groundbreaking book *Start with Why*. His central message is simple yet profound: People don't buy what you do, they buy *why* you do it.

In other words, the purpose behind your actions, the reason you get out of bed in the morning, drives more lasting success than simply chasing tasks, roles or titles.

At 50 and beyond, this principle becomes even more vital. Earlier in life, many women chose careers for practical reasons: financial security, raising a family, or climbing a predictable ladder of success.

But now, with decades of experience and wisdom, you have the opportunity to make choices guided by purpose rather than pressure. The Why becomes the compass that helps us avoid distraction, choose meaningful work, and feel a renewed sense of energy.

Sinek explains that communicating your Why doesn't just inspire others: it inspires you.

It taps into what neuroscientists call the 'limbic brain,' the part of our mind that governs emotions, decision-making, and loyalty. That's why people are drawn to leaders and businesses that clearly articulate their purpose. They're not just selling products or services; they're creating movements.

For a woman over 50 considering a new career path or training program, starting with Why helps to cut through the noise of endless options and stay anchored to what really matters.

Helen, 61: From numbers to meaning

Helen had spent decades as an accountant. She knew the numbers and could run the spreadsheets blindfolded, but after years of balancing books for others, she felt uninspired. When she finally sat down to explore her why, she realized that what had always lit her up was teaching people how to feel confident about their finances.

With that clarity, she transitioned into financial coaching for women in midlife, blending her skills with her deeper purpose. Today, Helen describes her work as the most meaningful she has ever done.

Brenda, 58: Traveling to experience

Brenda worked for years in the corporate travel industry. When the pandemic disrupted her career, she asked herself: "Why did I love this work in the first place?" Her answer wasn't about airline tickets or logistics; it was about helping people discover new experiences and connections.

With that reason in mind, she reinvented herself as a local tourism guide, creating curated cultural experiences in her city. Her work shifted, but her purpose remained intact.

Asking yourself, "What is my Why?" can feel daunting at first, but it often emerges from patterns in your life. Think about moments when you've felt most alive, times when people have thanked you, or the themes that have run like golden threads through your career.

That's where your Why lives.

When you align your training, career choices or business ideas with your Why, work becomes more than a paycheck; it becomes a calling, a vocation. And at this stage in life, that sense of calling is often the difference between burnout and joy.

Exercise: Discovering Your Why

Ask yourself these three questions and write freely, without editing:

1. What makes me feel most alive?
Think about the moments—in work, relationships, or hobbies—where you lose track of time and feel deeply

2. What impact do I want to have?
Imagine how others would describe your contribution. Do you want to inspire, support, create, solve problems, or lead change?

3. What legacy do I want to leave?
Fast-forward 20 years. Looking back, what would make you proud of how you spent your time and energy?

Now, review what you've written. Circle words or phrases that repeat, or that spark excitement in your chest. These are the threads of your Why.

Learn Less, Gain More: Choosing Training That Truly Transforms

For many women who are lifelong learners, including myself, it's tempting to jump into courses without connecting them to your goals. By the time you reach 50 and beyond, your time, energy, and resources are too valuable to waste on courses that look impressive but don't move you closer to your goals.

Training at this stage is not about collecting certificates; it's about making intentional choices that create momentum for the life and career you want now. The key is aligning your learning with your Why, your practical needs, and your long-term vision.

The first step is clarity. Ask yourself: Why am I considering this training? Is it to pivot to a new industry, sharpen your confidence in technology, grow a small business, or simply to reignite curiosity?

Having a clear purpose prevents distraction by courses that sound exciting but don't serve your bigger goals. For example, if you're dreaming of consulting in healthcare policy, a short course in health data analysis might be more valuable than a generic leadership certificate.

Equally important is to consider practicality. Will the training deliver skills you can apply right away? Practicality often makes the difference between knowledge that sits in a folder and skills that open doors.

Janine, 57: Short Course Results

Janine had been in education for decades but wanted to move into online tutoring. Instead of enrolling in a costly postgraduate degree, she took a 6-week digital education design course. Within 3 months, she was designing engaging online programs and earning a steady income from home. The shorter, practical course delivered immediate results.

Flexibility also matters. At this stage of life, you may be balancing caregiving, part-time work, or your health. Look for options that fit around your lifestyle, such as online programs, modular learning, or weekend intensives.

Sophia, 62: Flexible Training

Sophia had always dreamed of moving into wellness coaching. She chose a part-time certification program that allowed her to study in the evenings while caring for her elderly mother. Two years later, Sophia is running a small but thriving wellness practice, and the flexibility of her training made it possible.

Another powerful filter is Return on Investment (ROI). Think beyond financial return. Will this training open doors to meaningful work, expand your network, or give you the confidence to pursue your next step?

Arlene, 59: Doubled ROI

At mid-career, Arlene invested in a social media marketing course to promote her art online. While the course itself wasn't expensive, the ROI was significant: her paintings started selling on Instagram, and she doubled her income within a year.

Finally, trust your instincts. The best training doesn't just give you a certificate; it sparks excitement. If a course energizes you, feels aligned with your values, and builds on your experience, that's usually the right sign.

Your Next Move: A Step-by-Step Worksheet to Turn Training Dreams into Action

1: Clarify Your Why

What's my reason for taking this training?

- To pivot careers
- To update skills for current work
- To grow a business

- To build confidence (e.g., tech skills)
- Personal interest/passion

Write your reason here:

2: Alignment Check
Does this course align with my values, passions, and lifestyle?

Yes / No / Not Sure

Notes:

3: Practical Outcomes
What specific skills or knowledge will I gain?

Can I apply these skills immediately?

Yes / No

Notes:

4: Flexibility
Does the schedule suit my life?

Full-time / Part-time / Online / Self-paced

Will it create unnecessary stress?

Yes / No

Notes:

5: Investment Value

What is the cost (money & time)?

Is the potential return (income, opportunities, confidence) worth it?

Yes / No

Notes:

6: Excitement Factor

Does this training spark curiosity and motivation?

Yes / No

Notes:

Decision:

After reviewing, is this training the right next step for me?

Yes / No / Explore Alternatives

Ageless Learning: Unlocking the Power of Your Mind After 50

When you are learning in mid-life, it's no longer about obligation, but empowerment. You're not ticking boxes for someone else's approval; you're choosing growth on your own terms.

Training is simply a tool to help you move closer to the life and sustainable and meaningful career you want now.

I look at it this way: every new skill you gain is another key that can unlock opportunities.

It could be a course that helps you feel more confident with technology, a certification that opens doors in a new industry, or a workshop that reignites an old passion. The point isn't to start from scratch; it's to build on the wisdom and experience you already carry.

And here's the truth: you don't need every skill, every qualification, or every credential.

You only need the ones that matter to you. That's why clarity is so important, knowing what fits your values, passions, and lifestyle makes your learning journey lighter, more joyful, and more effective.

So, when you look at training opportunities, ask yourself: Does this excite me? Will it move me closer to the life I want? If the answer is yes, that's the kind of training worth saying yes to.

Learning at 50-plus isn't about proving yourself, it's about expanding yourself. And the best part? You get to decide what matters most.

Tech-Savvy, Not Stressed: How to Learn New Tech Without Losing Your Cool.

Technology can feel intimidating, especially when it seems to evolve faster every week.

But here's the truth: you don't need to know everything—you only need to know the tools that matter for your goals. The key is learning tech in a way that feels empowering, not overwhelming.

Start small. Instead of signing up for a dozen apps or courses at once, pick one tool or platform that will make the biggest difference in your work or lifestyle. Maybe it's Zoom for client calls, Canva for presentations, or LinkedIn for networking. Master one before moving on to the next.

Break learning into bite-sized steps. Spend 15–20 minutes a day experimenting, watching a tutorial, or asking questions.

This steady approach builds familiarity and confidence far more effectively than trying to cram everything in at once.

Don't be afraid to ask for help. Younger colleagues, tech-savvy friends, or even community classes can provide shortcuts and reassurance. Remember, asking for support is not a weakness; it's a smart strategy.

Most importantly, keep your focus on why you're learning. Technology isn't about gadgets or trends; it's about connection, efficiency, and opening doors. When you link learning a new tool directly to a goal, whether landing a client, running a business, or staying connected with family, it suddenly feels relevant and motivating.

With patience, practice, and purpose, technology becomes less of a barrier and more of a bridge to the opportunities waiting for you now.

Tech Confidence Checklist

1: Define Your "Why"

What do I want to achieve with this tool? (e.g., grow business, connect, save time)

How will it support my goals right now?

2: Choose One Tool at a Time

Pick a single platform/app/software to focus on.

Ignore distractions until I'm confident with this one.

3: Break It into Small Steps

Watch a short tutorial or demo.

Try one basic feature today.

Practice for 15–20 minutes daily.

Step 4: Create a Support System

Ask a friend, colleague, or family member to show me tips.

Join an online group or forum for quick answers.

Bookmark reliable How-To resources.

5: Track Small Wins

Celebrate each feature you learn (e.g., setting up Zoom, posting on LinkedIn).

Write down progress so you can see growth.

6: Apply It Immediately

Use the new skill in real life (send an email, host a call, design a post).

Notice how it makes life or work easier.

7: Repeat with the Next Tool

Affirmation: *"Once I'm comfortable, I'll move on to the next platform that supports my goals."*

✷ Key Takeaways: The Space Between Mastery and Curiosity: Where Second Acts Begin

Gaps Aren't Weaknesses—They're Signals. What feels like a missing skill is often pointing you toward your next growth edge.

Every Gap Hides a Gateway. By leaning into what you don't yet know, you unlock new opportunities and industries.

Your Skills Compound. The blend of what you've mastered and what you're learning now creates second-act power no one else can replicate.

Curiosity Is Your Currency. The willingness to stretch, retrain, and adapt is more valuable than any single credential.

Second Acts Aren't Smaller Acts. They're bolder, wiser, and fueled by a lifetime of experience, ready to be reimagined.

💡 CLAIRE'S TIP

"Start with Strengths First: Don't get overwhelmed by what you lack. Begin by anchoring yourself in the skills and experiences you already have."

PART TWO

Making Your Move

6

Professional Presence: The Makeover That Opens Doors

Plenty of women won't think twice about splurging on a new dress, booking a fresh color and cut, or hopping on a plane for a well-earned escape. But ask when they last updated their CV, and you'll likely get a blank stare. Somehow, refreshing our wardrobe or highlights can feel more urgent than refreshing the one document that could change our entire career and financial future.

This is remarkable, as it is the primary tool for generating income and prosperity. By 50, most professional women have invested heavily in their education (and maybe still paying HECS) and gained additional experience through courses, committees, volunteer work, networking and other opportunities.

I consider my CV (and my LinkedIn profile) to be living documents that constantly reflect a picture of my professional self, informing prospective clients and employers globally what I am up to at any time and how I can contribute to their success.

One of the most important considerations when either writing a CV or updating one is to consider it from the perspective of contribution. Of course, it will showcase your achievements and skills, but most of all, you need to develop a sense of how you have contributed and how you will do that for our next employers. It will really differentiate you as being a giver rather than an opportunist.

Secondly, without a CV that focuses on keywords and phrases that the reader is looking for, it will not get past the Applicant Tracking Systems (ATS) used by most companies. This platform scans CVs for relevant keywords. By tailoring your CV, you can incorporate keywords from the job description, increasing your chances of passing the ATS and reaching a human reader.

Hays is in the business of global recruitment, and this is what the company has to say about CVs:

"A CV should be a work in progress. And, just like your car, if you don't service it regularly, it won't perform as well as it could. Even if you're not looking to start a job search, it's worthwhile keeping your resume up to date. You are constantly gaining new skills, experiences, and successes in your current role – keeping your resume updated with these means that you're not only broadcasting an up-to-date list of skills and experiences to your network, but if a dream role does happen to appear – you'll be ready to apply.

Regular updates also ensure you have the most relevant details fresh in your mind at the time of writing. This can be important to avoid getting stuck behind a line of applicants for a role you want because they have their resume up to date."

Hays and other recruitment agencies are excellent resources for learning best practices in creating an eye-catching CV. If you haven't heard of the excellent job-hunting book *What Color is Your Parachute* by Richard Bolles, which is updated and re-released annually, now is the time to dive in. There is also an edition of *What Color is Your Parachute Guide to Rethinking Resumes*, which is essential reading.

You're Polished. Your CV Should Be, Too

We all know that it is illegal for employers to ask our age, yet an outdated CV may just be reflecting that you are outdated as well.

If your CV looks like it time-traveled from a decade ago, it can signal that you haven't kept up. Counter age bias by showcasing current, in-demand skills: digital literacy, social media savvy, and technical know-how. And ditch the old-school layout. Opt for a clean, modern design that's easy on the eyes—not cluttered with tired formatting.

Richard Bolles' books also offer strategies for combating ageism in job hunting by focusing on skills over tenure, promoting continuous learning to stay current, avoiding age-related language and outdated terms, and networking strategically to find hidden opportunities rather than relying on outdated methods. His book emphasizes self-assessment and targeted job searching to highlight your value and adaptability.

When I have worked with clients, I've often created several CVs to target different jobs by tailoring the content to each specific role and company. By using keywords from the job description and highlighting relevant skills and achievements, you can match the employer's needs.

Having multiple CVs is also beneficial if you're applying for roles in different industries or career paths, as it allows you to showcase a distinct set of qualifications for each application.

Finally, maintain a confident tone throughout, and include volunteer work or mentorship roles to showcase additional contributions and community engagement. A well-crafted CV that balances experience with modern skills demonstrates confidence, professionalism, and readiness for new opportunities, empowering women over 50 to stand out in competitive job markets.

Your LinkedIn Is Your Billboard—Make It Unforgettable

Just as your CV needs to be a living document, in today's professional world, your online presence is often the first impression you make. LinkedIn has become a powerful platform for women over 50 to showcase their expertise, connect with opportunities, and position themselves as leaders in their field.

Employers heavily rely on LinkedIn during recruitment; a majority of recruiters (93-95%) use the platform to find and screen candidates, with some reports indicating that 90% of recruiters use it at some stage of the hiring process. Employers view LinkedIn profiles to verify qualifications, assess professional experience alignment with a resume, and gauge cultural fit by looking at engagement, connections, and professional behavior.

Start by looking at your LinkedIn profile as your personal brand statement. Does it reflect who you are now, your current skills, passions, and direction, or does it still read like a CV from 10 years ago?

Updating your profile is about alignment: ensuring your digital presence reflects the confident, capable woman you've become.

Begin with your headline. Too often, women list only their job title, but your headline should tell a story. Think beyond labels like Consultant or Manager and instead highlight the value you bring. For example: *Helping small businesses grow through smart financial strategies* or *Career coach empowering women to thrive in midlife transitions.* A compelling headline attracts attention and sparks curiosity.

Next, ensure your summary is written in the first person and conveys both professionalism and personality. Share not only what you've done, but also what motivates you, what you stand for, and how you can help others. Add industry-relevant keywords to increase your visibility in searches.

Finally, consistency matters. Align your LinkedIn profile with other platforms—your website, professional bio, or even your email signature—so your message is clear and cohesive across the digital space. This builds credibility and trust.

Remember, LinkedIn isn't just for job seekers. It's a stage for sharing insights, publishing thought pieces, and expanding your influence. Optimizing your online presence positions you as relevant, visible, and ready for new opportunities.

Exercise: Rewrite Your LinkedIn Headline

Write your current headline:

Ask: Does this reflect the value I bring today?

Rewrite it to highlight your expertise + impact.

Test it: Would someone want to click to learn more?

From Boutique Owner to Media Mentor—The Accidental Reinvention

At 58, Christina had already pivoted once—from running a retail boutique to seeking more personal balance. Then came a broken foot, followed by an 'ugly' medical boot that sparked an idea: why not make it fashionable? She redesigned the medical boot with stylish accessories, teaching herself PR when money was tight.

Her revamped media pitches landed her a spot—and victory—on US entertainer Steve Harvey's *Top Inventor Competition*, earning $20,000 and a surge of visibility. Alongside media fame, she leaned hard into storytelling: launching the *Living Ageless and Bold* podcast, writing a syndicated travel column, and interviewing Oscar winners— all while championing reinvention for women 50 plus.

From Hand Model to Lawyer—Reinvention at 60

Elizabeth Barbour rewrote her career script in her mid-50s. After earlier roles as a hand model and real estate developer, she decided to pursue law at 54, motivated by a desire for deeper fulfillment. She studied, passed the bar on her second try, and joined the Legal Aid Society in Roanoke, Virginia.

Today, at 68, she serves as a family law advocate—especially for women in transition and survivors of domestic violence.

Her pivot was powered by purpose, not promotions, a clear reminder that it's never too late to shape your legacy.

Returner Program Success—The Power of Profile and Preparation

While not a single-person story, the Visible Start initiative is a UK-based program that trains mid-life women, who are often rendered invisible in the advertising and marketing industry, to re-enter the workforce by providing them with digital marketing skills and career opportunities.

Jane Evans, 59, author of *Invisible to Invaluable: Unleashing the Power of Midlife Women,* launched the initiative in the early 2000s. It partners with large organizations to offer a unique program designed to combat ageism and sexism, connecting experienced female talent with real jobs and helping to shrink the gender pay gap.

Participants go through an 8-week program that includes CV rewriting, LinkedIn optimization, and confidence-building training.

According to Visible Start, more than 30 women from the program landed roles at advertising agency sponsor WPP and many more found jobs elsewhere. Regardless of their outcome, all participants reported a renewed sense of hope and visible transformation—both in their profiles and presence.

There are some important lessons from the actions that all these women made to move their careers forward:

Profile Clarity Wins

Whether it's a CV for a legal job or a LinkedIn that reflects reinvention, clarity can command opportunity. Elizabeth's goal-driven CV and the returners' newly polished profile showcase how presentation matters.

Reinvention Is Strategic—Not Desperate

Each woman leaned into new skills—not in spite of her age, but because of it. Their profiles reframed experience as an asset, not baggage.

Visibility Begets Opportunity

From media appearances to structured returner courses, each example underlines how stepping into the spotlight—or onto a polished platform—turns potential into reality.

Mindset Shift Fuels the Story

These women didn't just find new roles—they crafted narratives. They leaned into value, growth, and agency. Their profiles reflect not who they were, but who they chose to become.

✦ Key Takeaways: Align Your Presence with Your Possibility

- **Your Presence Is Your First Impression.** LinkedIn, CVs, bios, and even email signatures quietly broadcast who you are—make sure they align with where you're headed, not just where you've been.

- **Small Tweaks Create Big Shifts.** Updating your headline, summary, and imagery on LinkedIn can instantly position you for fresh opportunities.

- **Tell a Future-Focused Story.** Don't just list past roles—frame them as stepping stones to your next chapter. Show how your experience adds value now.

- **Consistency Builds Credibility.** Align your online profiles, CV, and even how you introduce yourself in person. A unified message amplifies trust.

- **Visibility Drives Opportunity.** A polished, up to-date presence attracts the right people: recruiters, collaborators, clients, before you even reach out.

> ## 💡 CLAIRE'S TIP
>
> "Think of your professional presence like a shop window. If it's outdated or cluttered, people will pass by. But when you refresh it—clean, clear, and true to who you are today—you don't just attract attention, you attract the right attention."

7

The Power Web: Building and Using Networks That Elevate Life After 50

When I launched ConnectedWomen the world's first technology site for women and its accompanying newsletter in 2007, it was in direct response to a statistic I couldn't ignore. Global research from UK advertising agency, Saatchi, revealed that 6 out of 10 women were walking out of stores selling electrical appliances, not because they couldn't find what they needed, but because of the dismissive or condescending attitude of the male sales staff.

That insight lit a fire in me.

I believed and still do that women shouldn't have to tolerate being underestimated or talked down to. They should be able to walk into any store feeling informed, empowered, and confident enough to push past outdated stereotypes. Connected Women was created to arm them with the knowledge and tools to do just that.

It was natural for me to launch the platform through Australia's powerful and supportive women's networks. This experience also gave me the confidence to attend the Chicago Women's Marketing Conference at the Chicago Cultural Center. It was the world's premier conference on Marketing to Women (M2W), focusing on strategies and psychological insights for effective marketing to female audiences.

Here, I had the opportunity to network with female leaders, including Marti Barletta, author of Marketing To Women, the first book on the subject, which established Marti as the go-to authority on marketing to women. I was also able to share my experiences and best practices. It took my business and confidence to the next level.

By the time you have arrived at 50, your network is more valuable than ever. Over decades, you've built connections across industries, communities, and life stages, and the key now is learning how to tap into these relationships with confidence and purpose.

Networking at this stage isn't about collecting business cards or attending events out of obligation. It's about forming meaningful, strategic connections that align with your career vision. That might mean rekindling old professional relationships, joining groups that reflect your current interests, or building new circles in industries you're exploring.

Start by reviewing your existing network. Who do you already know that can open doors, offer advice, or simply encourage you? Many women discover that opportunities are just one or two conversations away. Reach out authentically— share your new direction, ask thoughtful questions, and express how you might also support them. Networking is reciprocal, not transactional.

Don't underestimate the power of digital networking. LinkedIn groups, online communities, and virtual events are excellent spaces to connect without the pressure of traditional networking. Posting insights or commenting on others' work also positions you as visible and engaged.

How COVID Supercharged Online Networking

Before COVID, networking often meant name tags, crowded rooms, and awkward small talk over canapés. But when the world shut down in 2020, so did traditional networking and in its place, something far more accessible and powerful took off : online networking.

Almost overnight, platforms like LinkedIn, Zoom, Slack, and Clubhouse became the new meeting grounds for professionals. Geographic barriers vanished. Suddenly, you could connect with an industry leader in London, a mentor in New York, or a collaborator in Singapore, all in the same week, without leaving your living room.

COVID didn't just shift how we networked—it redefined who could show up. For women, working parents, caregivers, introverts, and anyone previously excluded from the 'old boys' club-style events, online networking created a level playing field. With webcams on and filters off , people started showing up as their full selves, less polished, more real, an authenticity built stronger, faster connections.

Social media also took on a more intentional role. LinkedIn evolved from a static résumé site into a hub for thought leadership and conversation. Twitter Spaces (now X) and professional Facebook groups gained traction. Virtual conferences became smarter and more inclusive, with interactive breakout sessions, live chats, and networking lounges that mimicked real-world mingling.

And while some of this momentum has slowed with the return to in-person events, the legacy of COVID-powered networking is here to stay. Professionals now expect a hybrid approach, the freedom to connect online and offline, to build global relationships without geographic limits, and to grow their careers from wherever they are.

The result? A more democratized, more human way to network. One that's not just about who you know, but what you bring to the (virtual) table.

Finally, remember that building networks is about quality, not quantity. A handful of strong, supportive connections will always carry more weight than hundreds of weak ties. At this stage, your goal isn't just professional advancement—it's surrounding yourself with people who energize, inspire, and open new possibilities.

Exercise: Your Networking Action Plan

1. **Map your current network:** Write down 10 people you already know who could support or inspire your next step.

2. **Reconnect:** Choose two people to reach out to this week. Send a message, invite them for coffee, or schedule a Zoom call.

3. **Expand:** Identify one new group, event, or online community to join in the next month.

4. **Give first:** Ask yourself, "How can I support this person?" before asking for help.

Here's a friendly, professional reconnection script your readers can adapt for email or LinkedIn messages:

Reconnection Script

Subject line (if email): Great to reconnect!

Message:
Hi [Name],

I hope you're doing well. I was thinking about you recently and wanted to reach out. I'm in the process of exploring some new directions in my career/life, and it reminded me of the great conversations and insights we've shared in the past.

I'd love to catch up and hear what you're working on these days. If you're open to it, perhaps we could schedule a quick call or coffee over the next couple of weeks?

No pressure at all. I just value your perspective and thought it would be wonderful to reconnect.

Warm regards,
[Your Name]

Adaptations:
- If reaching out to someone in a professional context, you could add:
  "I'm especially interested in [industry/topic] right now and would love to hear your thoughts."

- If reaching out to an old friend/colleague, keep it warm:
  "It would be great to hear how life is going and share what's new with me, too."

This approach keeps things light, respectful, and authentic—showing genuine interest in the other person while subtly signaling your new direction.

Great Places to Grow Your Network at 50+

- **Professional Associations and Industry Groups**
  Join organizations related to your field or emerging industries you're curious about. Many host local meetups, conferences, and webinars where you can connect with like-minded professionals.

- **LinkedIn Groups and Online Communities**
  Participate in groups tailored to midlife professionals, women in leadership, or industry-specific spaces. Contributing insights and asking questions can quickly build your visibility and credibility.

- **Alumni Networks**
  Reconnect with your university, past workplaces, or training program alumni associations. Shared history creates instant rapport, and many of these networks actively support career transitions.

- **Co-Working Spaces and Local Business Hubs**
  Many cities have co-working spaces, business chambers, or innovation hubs that welcome professionals of all ages. These spaces encourage collaboration and offer events to meet entrepreneurs and consultants.

- **Interest-Based Communities**
  Don't underestimate the power of passion-based groups—book clubs, volunteer organizations, or wellness groups. Personal connections often lead to professional opportunities, especially when built on shared values.

Double Your Power: How to Turn Online and Offline Connections into Opportunities

The most powerful networks are built at the intersection of online and offline worlds. For women over 50, this blended approach opens doors to opportunities that may not be apparent through a single channel alone.

As discussed earlier, online platforms, LinkedIn, industry forums, and professional groups deliver visibility far beyond your immediate circle. They allow you to showcase your expertise, publish insights, and connect with people across industries and geographies. A well-curated online presence communicates your value clearly and consistently. But the true magic happens when you combine this digital reach with the authenticity of offline connection.

Offline networking still holds incredible weight. Coffee chats, industry events, and local meetups allow you to create a personal bond that digital communication can't fully replicate. Face-to-face interactions build trust more quickly and leave a stronger, lasting impression. They also give you a chance to read body language, engage in deeper conversations, and build relationships that feel more human and memorable.

The key is not to treat online and offline networks as separate silos, but as complementary. For example, you might first connect with someone on LinkedIn, then invite them for coffee when you're in the same city. Or you might meet someone at a conference and later follow up by engaging with their posts online. Each channel reinforces the other, creating a loop of visibility and trust.

At this stage in life, your time is precious—so focus on relationships that feel mutually energizing. Use online tools to expand your reach, but lean on offline interactions to deepen the bonds. When used together, these two approaches create a powerful network that supports your career, learning, and your growth in the years ahead.

Blending Strategy: From Online to Offline (and Back Again)

- Connect on LinkedIn, join relevant groups, or comment thoughtfully on someone's post.
- Send a personalized message when connecting: mention a shared interest, event, or article.

Deepen the Connection Offline

- If local, invite them for coffee or to an industry meetup.
- If not local, suggest a short Zoom/phone call. Keep it light and exploratory.

Follow Up Online

- After the offline interaction, engage with their content, congratulate them on milestones, or share relevant resources.
- Post a thank-you note (private or public, depending on comfort).

Keep the Loop Alive

- Alternate between online engagement (likes, comments, shares) and occasional offline touchpoints (catch-ups, events).
- Aim for quarterly reconnections—enough to stay visible without overwhelming either side.

Give Before You Ask

- Share an article they'd value, introduce them to someone in your network, or support their work.
- Relationships grow stronger when they're reciprocal.

From Quiet Corners to Confident Connections: Overcoming Shyness After 50

I know many mature, lovely women for whom the idea of networking or putting themselves 'out there' in the business world can feel uncomfortable. Perhaps you've always been more reserved, or maybe you're carrying the weight of self-doubt that crept in over the years—thoughts like "I don't want to bother anyone" or "What if I don't have enough to offer?" The truth is, shyness and hesitation are completely normal feelings, but they don't have to hold you back.

First, recognize that most people appreciate genuine connection. Reaching out isn't an intrusion—it's an opportunity for both sides to learn, share, and grow. Think of networking not as 'selling yourself,' but as building relationships rooted in curiosity and generosity. Shifting your perspective from "What can I get?" to "What can I give?" reduces pressure and makes interactions more natural.

Second, preparation helps dissolve anxiety. If walking into a room of strangers feels overwhelming, set a simple goal: introduce yourself to two people, or ask one thoughtful question. Online, you might start by liking posts, leaving short comments, or sharing articles before sending a direct message. Small steps add up to confidence.

Third, remember that your life experience is a powerful asset. You bring wisdom, resilience, and perspective that others value deeply—even if you underestimate it yourself. When you show up authentically, people respond to your warmth, not perfection.

Finally, treat networking like a skill, not a personality trait. With practice, you'll grow more comfortable. Confidence doesn't come before action—it comes because of it. Every conversation builds momentum, and every small win strengthens your self-belief.

Exercise: Confidence in Action

1. **Reframe:** Write down three limiting thoughts you have about networking (e.g., *"I'm not interesting enough"*). Next to each one, rewrite it as an empowering truth (e.g., *"I have unique experiences worth sharing"*).

2. **Micro-Step:** Commit to one small action this week—comment on a LinkedIn post, introduce yourself at a local event, or send a friendly reconnection message.

3. **Reflect:** Afterward, jot down how it felt and what you learned. Noticing the positives builds confidence for next time.

Icebreaker Questions for Networking Success:

For Professional Settings (conferences, events, networking groups):
1. "What brought you to this event today?"
2. "I noticed you work in [industry/role]—what do you enjoy most about it?"
3. "What trends are you seeing in your field right now?"
4. "How did you get started in your career?"
5. "I'd love to hear about any projects you're excited about at the moment."

For Casual or Social Settings (meetups, coffee chats):
1. "How do you usually spend your weekends?"
2. "Have you read or listened to anything interesting lately?"
3. "What's something you're enjoying working on right now, personal or professional?"
4. "What drew you to join this group/event?"
5. "What's been the highlight of your week so far?"

For Reconnecting Online (LinkedIn messages, emails):
1. "I came across your recent post on [topic] it was really insightful! What inspired it?"
2. "I noticed we're both interested in [industry/trend]. What are your thoughts on how it's evolving?"
3. "It's been a while since we last connected—what's new and exciting for you these days?"

✨ Key Takeaways: From Clicks to Coffee: Redefining Connection for a New Era of Work

- **Networking Is Hybrid Now.** Success comes from weaving together both your digital presence and in-person relationships. One without the other leaves opportunities on the table.

- **Online Builds Reach.** LinkedIn, social media, and virtual groups expand your visibility far beyond your immediate circle—opening doors to people you'd never meet otherwise.

- **Offline Builds Trust.** Coffee chats, events, and face-to-face moments cement credibility in a way digital alone cannot.

- **Consistency Matters.** Show up with the same story, tone, and energy online as you do offline—this alignment amplifies your personal brand.

- **Leverage the Loop.** Move fluidly between both worlds: take online conversations offline (over coffee, on Zoom, at events) and bring offline encounters online (connect, share, and endorse). That's where momentum builds.

💡 CLAIRE'S TIP

"Don't think of online and offline networking as two separate strategies. Think of them as a loop. The magic happens when you move easily between the two, turning a like into a lunch, and a handshake into a headline on LinkedIn."

8

Beyond CVs: Navigating the New Job Hunt with Confidence and Purpose

Gone are the days when looking for work meant scanning the classifieds, mailing out CVs, and waiting for a polite phone call. I remember walking the streets in my local suburb when I was 16, looking for a casual job and asking shop owners if they needed anyone!

Today's job hunt is a very different game; digital-first, fast-moving and heavily shaped by technology. For women over 50, this can feel intimidating at first glance. Applicant tracking systems, LinkedIn algorithms, online interviews—none of these existed when many of us first started our careers.

But here's the truth: the new job market isn't stacked against you. In fact, it offers more opportunities than ever for women with experience, resilience and adaptability. The key lies in learning the rules of this new landscape and reframing your decades of skills into the language of today's workplace.

This chapter is about showing you how. It's about proving that age is not a barrier, but a powerful asset, if you know how to present yourself. Whether you're seeking a full-time role, exploring part-time opportunities, or pivoting into a fresh industry, the modern job hunt can become less of a hurdle and more of a launchpad.

Digital-first applications. Most employers now use online platforms, job boards, and applicant tracking systems (ATS) to filter candidates. That means your résumé may be read by software before it ever reaches a human. Keywords, clear formatting, and tailored applications are critical to getting noticed.

Online presence matters. Hiring managers routinely check LinkedIn, and sometimes other platforms, to verify your expertise and personality fit. Your profile is no longer optional—it's an extension of your résumé. Showcasing skills, achievements, and even recommendations online is part of being taken seriously as a candidate.

Skills over titles. While traditional job titles still matter, many employers now value demonstrated skills and adaptability just as much. Transferable skills such as communication, problem solving, leadership, are often what makes a candidate stand out, especially in industries undergoing rapid change.

Networking is central. Research shows most opportunities are filled through networks rather than job ads. Today, personal connections and referrals carry more weight than ever. Being visible to your network can open doors that applications alone might not.

Age awareness. While ageism exists, many employers are also recognizing the value of experienced professionals. The key is presenting yourself as adaptable, tech-savvy, and forward-looking—showing that your years of experience are an asset, not a limitation.

The hiring process has changed, yes, but so have you. With your experience, resilience, and wisdom, you're in a strong position to approach this new landscape strategically. Think of it less as a challenge and more as an exciting opportunity to align your next chapter with who you are now.

Karen 54: Pivoting into Tech

At 54, Karen, a former project manager, felt invisible when sending out CVs. After reskilling with a digital marketing certificate, she highlighted her transferable skills of organisation, leadership, and communication on LinkedIn. Within months, she landed a role at a start-up, where her calm presence in high-pressure situations was seen as invaluable.

Monica 57: Returning After a Career Break

Monica, 57, had stepped back from full-time work to care for her parents. When she was ready to return, she faced bias around her "employment gap." She reframed it as a period of growth, managing complex caregiving responsibilities, volunteering, and completing an online governance course. A not-for-profit hired her into a leadership role, impressed by her breadth of skills.

Elizabeth 62: Networking Opens the Door

Elizabeth, 62, applied online for months with little success. Then she focused on networking—reaching out to former colleagues, attending alumni events, and posting thoughtful insights on LinkedIn. A connection introduced her to a recruiter, and soon she secured a part-time strategy role that perfectly balanced her lifestyle and expertise.

Exercise: Audit Your Job Hunt Toolkit

The hiring process may feel different now, but you already have the raw materials to succeed. This exercise will help you take stock of what's working and where to update your approach.

Step 1: Review Your CV

- Does it highlight skills and achievements, not just job titles and duties?
- Is it tailored toward the types of roles you're seeking now, not the roles you had 10 years ago?
- Does it use clear formatting that an ATS (Applicant Tracking System) can read (simple fonts, no graphics, keyword alignment)?

Step 2: Audit Your LinkedIn Profile

- Headline: Does it clearly show your current value and direction, or does it read like your last job title?
- Summary: Does it tell your story in a warm, confident way?
- Activity: Are you visible: liking, commenting and sharing insights, so your profile looks current and engaged?

Step 3: Check Your Online Presence

- Google yourself. What shows up? Does it reflect the professional image you want to convey?
- Do you need to clean up, update, or add visibility on other platforms (e.g., portfolio site, professional association profiles)?

Step 4: Assess Your Network

- Who are the five people you could reconnect with this month?
- Who in your network works in industries or roles that interest you now?
- Are you giving as much as you're asking (sharing resources, offering help, congratulating others)?

Step 5: Create Your Action List

- Write down three specific updates you'll make this week—whether it's rewriting your CV headline, refreshing your LinkedIn photo, or sending a reconnection message.

Flipping the Script: Turning Ageism into Your Interview Advantage

Let's be honest: ageism exists. Some employers may carry outdated assumptions that people over 50 are less adaptable, less tech-savvy, or less ambitious. While frustrating, these biases don't define your worth, or your opportunities. What matters is how you present yourself, the energy you bring, and the strategies you use to highlight your strengths.

In your applications: Tailor your CV to focus on skills, achievements, and results rather than long job histories. You don't need to list every role from the 1980s or 1990s—summarize early experience and emphasize the past 10 years at the most. Use current terminology and showcase digital tools you've worked with. This demonstrates that you're up to date and adaptable.

In your interviews: Employers may sometimes ask questions that hint at concerns about age, such as your ability to learn new systems or fit into a younger team. Instead of reacting defensively, confidently reframe your answer. For example:

- If asked about technology, share how you've recently learned and applied new tools.
- If asked about teamwork, highlight your ability to collaborate across generations and mentor younger colleagues.
- If asked about long-term plans, express enthusiasm for contributing and growing with the organization in meaningful ways.

Mindset matters. Walk into interviews with the belief that your age is not a liability but a unique advantage. Your resilience, judgment, and experience give you a perspective that younger candidates simply cannot replicate. Show curiosity, flexibility, and a forward-looking attitude—qualities that challenge stereotypes and build trust.

Leverage your value. Many organizations are beginning to recognize the strengths of experienced professionals: loyalty, stability, and deep expertise. By confidently positioning yourself as adaptable, skilled, and committed, you remind employers that hiring you is not just filling a role, it's investing in someone who will deliver lasting impact.

Ageism may exist, but it doesn't define you. With strategy, confidence, and authenticity, you can turn bias into an opportunity to shine.

Exercise: Reframe Your Story

This exercise helps you turn potential ageist assumptions into powerful, confident responses that highlight your strengths.

Step 1: Identify Common Assumptions

Write down three concerns you think an employer might have about hiring someone over 50. Examples:

- "She might not be comfortable with new technology."
- "He won't fit into a younger team."
- "She's too close to retirement to invest in."

Step 2: Craft Reframes

Now, reframe each assumption into a strength. For example:

- Tech concern → *"I've recently mastered [specific software/app] and enjoy keeping up with tools that make work more efficient."*

- Team dynamic → *"I thrive in multi-generational teams—I bring mentoring experience while also learning from younger colleagues."*

- Retirement worry → *"I'm looking for a role where I can contribute meaningfully over the next several years and continue to grow professionally."*

Step 3: Practice Out Loud

Say your reframed responses out loud until they feel natural and confident. This builds muscle memory so that if an interview question feels loaded, you already know how to pivot it into a strength.

Step 4: Add Your Own Example

Think of a real situation where you overcame one of these stereotypes (learning a new tool, collaborating across age groups, adapting to change). Use it as a short story in interviews—it's more persuasive than theory.

Scripts: Handling Tricky Interview Questions

Interviews can be nerve-wracking at any age, but for women over 50, some questions may feel especially loaded. Employers may not ask directly about age, but they sometimes probe around areas like technology skills, energy levels, or long-term commitment. Having strong, prepared responses will help you feel confident and in control.

Question 1: "Are you comfortable with new technology?"

What they might really be asking: "Can you keep up with today's tools?"

Scripted Response:

"I love learning new systems. In my last role, I quickly picked up [specific software or app], which became central to our workflow. I enjoy finding ways technology can make work more efficient."

Question 2: "Do you see yourself staying in this role long-term?"

What they might really be asking: "Are you too close to retirement?"

Scripted Response:

"I'm looking for a role where I can make a strong contribution over the coming years. I bring both experience and commitment, and I'm excited to grow with an organization that values those qualities."

Question 3: "How do you feel about working with a younger team or manager?"

What they might really be asking: "Will you fit in with younger colleagues?"

Scripted Response:

"I've worked with diverse teams throughout my career, including many younger colleagues, and I really enjoy the exchange of ideas across generations. I learn as much from them as they do from me."

Question 4: "You have a lot of experience—aren't you overqualified for this role?"

What they might really be asking: "Will you get bored or leave quickly?"

Scripted Response:

"My experience allows me to contribute value quickly, but what excites me about this role is [specific aspect of the job]. I'm motivated by the opportunity to [impact, growth, or contribution], which makes this role an excellent fit."

Exercise: Write Your Own Interview Scripts

The best way to feel confident in interviews is to prepare in advance. Use this exercise to create your own scripts for the questions you most worry about.

Step 1: Identify Your Triggers

Think about the interview questions that make you nervous. Write down at least three. These could be:

- "Why did you leave your last role?"
- "How do you keep your skills up to date?"
- "What are your salary expectations?"

2. Ask yourself: *What is the employer really trying to find out?* For example:

- Concern: "Are your skills current?"
- Concern: "Will you be satisfied with this role long-term?"
- Concern: "Can we afford you?"

3. Write a short, confident script (2–3 sentences) that addresses the concern while highlighting your value. Example:

- Concern: "Are your skills current?"
- Script: *"I regularly invest in my learning. For example, I recently completed [training/course], and I enjoy staying on top of industry changes."*

4: Practice Out Loud

Say your scripts until they sound natural. Imagine the interviewer asking you the question, then confidently deliver your response.

5: Keep a Script Bank

Store your answers in a notebook or document. Update them as you gain new experiences, training, or achievements.

✿ Key Takeaways: You're More Than a CV. You're a Story in Motion

- **The CV Isn't the Whole Story.** Employers and collaborators look for authenticity, alignment, And presence across multiple channels, not just bullet points on paper.

- **Purpose Is Magnetic.** When you're clear on *why* you want the role or industry, your energy and confidence come through in every interaction.

- **Your Network Is Your Secret Weapon.** Most opportunities are unlocked through connections, conversations, and referrals—not job boards.

- **Your Story Matters More Than Your Titles.** Framing your experience as a journey of growth and impact makes you memorable beyond credentials.

- **Confidence Is Contagious.** People respond to clarity and conviction, when you own your value, others see it too.

💡 CLAIRE'S TIP

"Think of the job hunt as storytelling, not selling. Your resume is just a brochure, but your conversations, presence and purpose are what truly land opportunities."

9

Boardroom Breakthroughs: Why Women Over 50 Are the Leaders the Future Needs

In many ways, women over 50 are the untapped powerhouse of leadership. At this stage in life, you bring a unique blend of professional expertise, life experience, resilience, and perspective that is invaluable to organizations and boards. Yet, despite these capabilities, women in this demographic remain underrepresented in senior leadership positions and boardrooms worldwide. Breaking through these barriers requires both systemic change within organizations and personal strategies that empower women to claim the influence they deserve.

This chapter explores the opportunities, challenges, and strategies for women over 50 to move upward into senior leadership and board roles, demonstrating that the second half of life can be the strongest and most impactful stage of a career.

Women who have reached midlife bring a compelling mix of qualities to senior leadership and governance roles.

- **Depth of Experience:** With decades of professional and personal experience, they understand industries, markets, and people at a level that only comes with time.

- **Emotional Intelligence:** Years of managing careers, families, and community responsibilities foster strong interpersonal skills, conflict resolution, and mentoring abilities.

- **Resilience:** Women over 50 have often navigated career transitions, biases, and personal challenges, equipping them with resilience essential for complex leadership.

- **Perspective:** At this stage, ego-driven ambition is often replaced by a focus on impact, purpose, and Legacy. These are qualities that align closely with the needs of boards and purpose-driven leadership.

Organizations seeking stability, foresight, and wisdom can greatly benefit from tapping into this talent pool.

The Current Landscape: Progress and Gaps

Progress has been made toward greater female representation in leadership and board roles, but gaps remain. Globally, women hold around 20–30% of board seats, depending on the region, and representation drops further when focusing on women over 50.

While specific data on the percentage of board seats held by women over 50 in Australia is not readily available in recent reports; however, data for Australian Government boards (54.4% women directors as of June 2024) and ASX 300 boards (37.5% women directors as of June 2025) show overall gender representation but do not break down by age. The average age of an ASX 300 director is around 61, with female directors being slightly younger on average at 58.7

Ageism intersects with gender bias, creating a double hurdle.

- **Corporate Boards:** Many companies set quotas or targets for women on boards, yet too often the selection skews toward younger executives perceived as more "dynamic."

- **Executive Leadership:** Women over 50 may face assumptions about nearing retirement, despite often having 15–30 productive years ahead.

- **Nonprofit and Public Boards:** While women are better represented here, these roles are sometimes unpaid or less influential.

The reality is that women over 50 remain an underutilized leadership resource, and breaking through requires dismantling biases and reframing what effective leadership looks like.

From Influence to Impact: Proven Strategies for Stepping into Senior Leadership and Board Roles

- **Reframe Midlife as a Career Peak**. Women over 50 need to see and position themselves as being at the height of their value. This is not a winding-down stage, but a phase of maximum contribution. Updating personal narratives, LinkedIn profiles, and professional conversations to reflect this sense of momentum is critical.

- **Build and Leverage Networks.** Networking is no longer optional; it is the engine that drives board and leadership appointments. Women should: Reconnect with past colleagues and mentors. Join professional associations and leadership networks. Actively seek sponsors who can advocate for them in boardroom selection processes.

- **Acquire Board-Readiness Skills.** Boards require specific competencies: governance, financial literacy, risk management, and strategic oversight. Women aspiring to board roles should consider:
    - Board-readiness programs and certifications.
    - Mentorship from experienced directors.
    - Volunteering for nonprofit boards as stepping stones.

Showcase Transferable Value. Experience in operational leadership, crisis management, stakeholder engagement, or transformation initiatives should be framed as strategic assets for boards and senior leadership roles. Translating achievements into measurable outcomes strengthens positioning.

- **Embrace Technology and Lifelong Learning.** To counter stereotypes of being "out of touch," women must remain digitally literate and curious learners. Engaging with emerging trends such as AI, ESG, and digital transformation signals relevance and foresight.

- **Cultivate Confidence and Executive Presence.** Securing senior roles often comes down to presence and confidence. Women can:
    - Practice concise, impactful communication.
    - Demonstrate authority without apology.
    - Own their expertise and stop underselling achievements.

Success Stories: Trailblazers Over 50

Countless women over 50 have risen to top leadership and board roles, reshaping industries and organizations. Examples include:

- **Christine Lagarde,** now President of the European Central Bank, assumed her most powerful role after 60.

- **Julia Gillard,** Australia's first female Prime Minister, now 59, sits on multiple Australian and global boards and co-authored with Ngozi Okonjo-Iweala *Leadership: Real Lives, Real Lessons' in 2020.*

- **Indra Nooyi,** former CEO of PepsiCo, joined multiple boards post-CEO career.

- **Nonprofit leaders and entrepreneurs such as Adriana Huffington and Melinda Gates** who pivoted careers after 50, demonstrating that reinvention can lead directly into boardrooms.

These stories reinforce that women can ascend to their most impactful leadership roles later in life.

Step Into Power Gracefully—Practical Steps at Your Own Pace

Audit Your Career Capital: List achievements, skills, networks, and influence you bring.

Update Your Brand: Refresh LinkedIn, CV, and personal website to highlight leadership impact.

Seek Sponsorship: Identify influential allies who can open boardroom doors.

Invest in Board Education: Enroll in programs that build governance and director *skills.*

Practice the Pitch: *Be ready to articulate in two minutes why you're board-ready.*

Stay Visible: *Publish thought leadership, speak at conferences, and share insights online.*

✨ Key Takeaways: Moving Up into Senior Leadership and Board Roles

1. **Midlife is a Peak, Not a Plateau**
   Women over 50 bring unmatched depth of experience, resilience, and perspective to leadership roles, this stage of life is often when your influence is strongest.

2. **Visibility and Networks Matter**
   Leadership and board opportunities often come through trusted networks and sponsorship. Cultivating visibility and strong advocates is as important as your CV.

3. **Board-Readiness is a Skillset**
   Governance, financial literacy, and risk management are core competencies. Gaining certifications, mentorship, or nonprofit board experience helps position you as board-ready.

4. **Age + Gender Bias Can Be Overcome**
   Ageism and stereotypes exist, but reframing your value as future-focused, tech-literate, and purpose-driven helps dismantle assumptions.

5. **Leadership is About Legacy**
   This stage isn't only about career advancement—it's about leaving an impact, mentoring others, and shaping industries and communities for the future.

♀ CLAIRE'S TIP

"Think of yourself not as 'competing' for a seat at the table, but as *bringing something indispensable* to it. Your wisdom, judgment, and perspective are assets no algorithm or younger candidate can replicate. Position yourself with confidence: you're not winding down; you're stepping up to influence where it matters most."

10

Unleashing the Second Act: How Women Over 50 Turn Creativity into Prosperity

Ayurveda, the ancient Indian system of medicine developed over 3,000 years ago, offers a radically different lens through which to view health, aging, and life transitions—especially for women. Rooted in the belief that true wellness comes from balance between the body, mind, and spirit, Ayurveda doesn't treat menopause as a decline or medical condition to be "managed." Instead, it honors it as a powerful natural milestone.

According to Ayurvedic philosophy, menopause, which typically occurs around the age of 50, is not an end, but a beginning. It marks the shift into a new phase of life, one where a woman's energy turns inward, making space for renewed clarity, insight, and creativity. Rather than being defined by loss (of fertility or youth), this stage is seen as a time of deep wisdom, personal growth, and spiritual expansion.

Ayurveda also offers tools to support this transition gently and holistically. Through mindful nutrition, herbs, yoga, meditation, and daily rituals, it helps women maintain equilibrium during hormonal shifts. The focus is not just on easing physical symptoms like hot flashes or insomnia, but on fostering emotional resilience and reconnecting with one's deeper purpose.

In a world that often sidelines older women or frames menopause in purely medical terms, Ayurveda provides a refreshing, empowering narrative: that this stage of life is not something to fear or fix, but a sacred turning point, vanaprastha ashram—a chance to realign with who you truly are and how you want to live going forward.

With the childbearing years behind you, the powerful energy that has been the domain of the reproductive and child-rearing years can now be channeled into a different form of creativity.

For women over 50, creativity can become a powerful second act, not just as a hobby or outlet, but as the foundation of prosperous careers. At this stage of life, many women find themselves asking, "What do I want to do with my time, talent, and energy now?" For an increasing number of people, the answer lies in creativity.

From writing books and launching art studios, to opening design businesses, teaching workshops, or building online creative platforms, women are proving that it is not too late to turn imagination into income. In fact, the midlife and later years may be the most fertile time for creative prosperity.

Why Creativity Blooms After 50

Life Experience Becomes Raw Material. By the time women reach their 50s, they have lived through decades of stories, challenges, and triumphs. This reservoir of experience becomes the raw material for art, writing, design, music, or any creative pursuit. A painting might carry the depth of a lifetime's emotions. A memoir or podcast may draw on stories that resonate across generations. Creativity becomes richer because it is infused with perspective.

Confidence to Be Authentic. Many women discover that after 50, they care less about external judgment and more about self-expression. Freed from earlier worries about 'fitting in,' they create from a place of authenticity. This confidence leads to bold choices, unique voices, and work that stands out in crowded creative spaces.

A Shift in Priorities. The years after 50 often bring a shift from building careers or raising families to focusing on meaning, impact, and legacy. Creativity offers a path to fulfillment and, importantly, the freedom to choose projects that align with personal values.

Technology as a Gateway. Digital platforms have revolutionized creative careers. Whether through Etsy, Instagram, YouTube, Substack, or self-publishing, women can now bypass traditional gatekeepers and reach audiences directly. Technology has democratised access to markets, making it easier than ever to monetise creativity.

The Hidden Hurdles: Why the Creative Path Tests You Before It Transforms You

One of the biggest internal barriers women face is the belief that it's too late to start. Decades of conditioning may whisper, "Creative careers belong to the young." The reality is that creativity knows no age limit. Self-doubt must be replaced with the recognition that lived experience is a strength, not a weakness.

Another common concern is whether creative work can be profitable. For many women, creativity has often been relegated to a hobby rather than a career. Shifting the mindset from hobbyist to creative entrepreneur is essential. Prosperity is possible, but it requires treating creativity as both art and business.

Women who have kept their creative passions private may find the idea of self-promotion daunting. Yet visibility is non-negotiable in creative industries. Building an audience, sharing work, and embracing marketing are skills that can be learned and doing so allows women to claim the recognition they deserve.

The digital landscape moves quickly, and the thought of mastering online tools, platforms, and marketing can feel overwhelming. But learning is lifelong, and resources abound. From free tutorials to mentorship programs, skill-building is accessible to anyone willing to engage.

From Passion to Prosperity: Unlocking the Pathways to a Creative Career That Thrives

Turning Hobbies into Businesses. Many women discover that passions pursued for years can become income streams. A painter might sell her art online; a knitter may open an Etsy shop; a gardener could develop a consulting or content business. The key is to shift perspective: if others value the work, it has market potential.

Freelancing and Consulting. Creative services, such as writing, graphic design, photography, editing, or music instruction, can translate into freelance careers. Platforms like Upwork, Fiverr, Freelance, and LinkedIn provide global marketplaces for skilled creatives, while local networks offer opportunities closer to home.

Content Creation. The digital era has made creators of us all. Substack newsletters, podcasts, YouTube channels, and Instagram platforms allow women to share creative voices directly with audiences. Monetization comes through subscriptions, sponsorships, and community building.

Teaching and Mentoring. After decades of honing skills, many women find fulfillment in teaching others. Online courses, workshops, and coaching programs allow creatives to package expertise and share it while generating income.

Collaborative Ventures. Collaboration can multiply opportunity. Joint projects with other creatives — exhibitions, anthologies, performances, or partnerships — expand networks and visibility while sharing resources.

Develop a Creative Identity. Moving into a prosperous creative career requires more than talent; it requires a clear identity. Ask: What am I creating? Who is it for? What value does it offer? Defining this identity helps with branding, marketing, and positioning.

Prosperity rarely happens overnight. Begin with manageable projects, such as a blog post, a small collection, or a short course, and build consistency. Momentum comes from showing up regularly and steadily expanding.

Creativity also thrives when paired with entrepreneurship. Learn the basics of pricing, branding, contracts, and marketing. Treat creative work with the same professionalism as any other career.

Build a Digital Presence. A website, social media presence, and online portfolio are essential. These platforms are modern galleries, publishers, and stages. They allow work to be seen, shared, and purchased globally.

Create Multiple Income Streams. Diversifying revenue protects against instability. For example, a writer may combine book sales with speaking engagements, workshops, and online courses. A visual artist might sell original works, prints, and teach classes. Multiple streams ensure sustainability.

Stay Curious and Keep Learning. Engage with new tools, trends, and platforms. Whether learning to market on TikTok, exploring AI in design, or experimenting with new mediums, curiosity keeps creativity fresh and relevant.

Here are some inspiring examples of women who built (or reinvented) creative careers after 50. These are real women, well-known and lesser-known, who prove that creativity doesn't expire with age; it evolves.

Visual Arts & Design

- **Julia Child** – The beloved chef and TV personality didn't publish her first cookbook, *Mastering the Art of French Cooking*, until she was 49, and launched her television career at 51—becoming a global icon for reinvention through passion and persistence.

- **Carmen Herrera** – A Cuban-American painter who worked quietly for decades. She sold her first painting at age 89 and had her first solo museum exhibition at 101.

Writing & Literature

- **Laura Ingalls Wilder** – Published her first *Little House* book in her 60s, launching one of the most beloved children's series ever.

- **Toni Morrison** – Although she began publishing in her late 30s, Morrison didn't receive her Nobel Prize in Literature until her 60s, proving that literary recognition can blossom later in life.

- **Mary Wesley** – Published her first adult novel at 57 and went on to write 10 bestsellers, becoming one of Britain's most popular authors in her later years.

Music & Performance

- **Sharon Jones** – Worked as a corrections officer and armored car guard before launching her soul singing career in her 40s. By 50, she was touring globally with Sharon Jones & The Dap-Kings.

- **Susan Boyle** – Became a worldwide star at 47 on *Britain's Got Talent* and launched an international singing career that flourished well into her 50s and beyond.

Film & Television

- **Phyllida Lloyd** – Directed *Mamma Mia!* (2008) and *The Iron Lady* (2011), achieving her biggest successes as a film director in her 50s.

- **Kathryn Bigelow** – Although she had directed films earlier, she became the first woman to win the Academy Award for Best Director at the age of 57 for *The Hurt Locker*.

Entrepreneurship & Creative Innovation

- **Vera Wang** – Worked in fashion journalism before becoming a bridal designer at 40. Her business exploded in her 50s, making her one of the world's most recognized designers.

- **Martha Stewart** – Built her brand empire later in life, with much of her influence and recognition skyrocketing in her 50s and beyond.

For women over 50, the path to prosperous creative careers is not just about financial gain. It is about expression, freedom, reinvention, and impact. This stage of life provides the perfect combination of wisdom, resilience, and authenticity to build something meaningful and lasting.

Creativity does not diminish with age, it deepens. The world needs the voices, perspectives, and artistry of women in midlife and beyond. Whether through painting, writing, music, design, or digital content, the second act of life can be the most creative—and the most prosperous.

The invitation is clear: if creativity is calling, answer it boldly. This is not the time to shrink back. This is the time to step forward, create, and prosper.

Creative Prosperity Roadmap: Turning Your Talent into Income After 50

Claim Your Creative Identity
- Stop calling it a hobby. Name yourself: writer, painter, designer, coach, storyteller, musician.
- Write down your creative strengths and the skills you want to highlight.

Mindset shift: You're not "dabbling." You're building.

Choose Your Prosperity Path
Decide how you want your creativity to generate value:

- **Products:** books, art, crafts, courses, photography.
- **Services:** consulting, coaching, workshops, speaking.
- **Platforms:** newsletters, YouTube, podcasts, social media communities.

Pick one starting point. Don't spread yourself too thin.

Build Your Portfolio (Proof of Value)
- Collect samples, testimonials, or pilot projects.
- If you're new, start with a small paid offer—even $50 for your first client shifts energy from "free" to "professional."
- Share your work publicly consistency builds credibility.

Price With Power, Not Apology
- Research market rates for your industry.
- Factor in your decades of experience—not just hours worked.
- Start higher than you think. Clients respect confidence.

Remember: You're charging for transformation, not just time.

Leverage Technology to Amplify Reach
- Create a simple website or portfolio page.
- Use platforms like Substack, Etsy, Fiverr, or Patreon, depending on your niche.
- Build an email list—your direct line to an audience who values you.

Technology removes gatekeepers. Use it.

Network With Intention

- Surround yourself with other creatives who are thriving. Energy is contagious.
- Collaborate: co-host events, cross-promote, guest post.
- Share your story, women over 50 inspire others simply by showing it's possible.

Protect Your Energy

- Schedule creative time like a non-negotiable meeting.
- Set boundaries with clients, family, and distractions.
- Balance prosperity with joy—remember, you're doing this for freedom, not burnout.

Scale What Works

- Once your first offer gains traction, expand by creating packages, products, or recurring income streams.
- Think long-term: How can this creative path sustain you for years to come?

✨ Key Takeaways: How Women Over 50 Turn Creativity into Prosperity

1. **Experience Is Your Edge**
   Decades of lived wisdom, resilience, and perspective fuel richer, more authentic creative work that resonates deeply.

2. **Age Brings Clarity**
   By 50, you know your values, your strengths, and what no longer serves you—creativity flows stronger when you're creating on your own terms.

3. **Creativity Is Currency**
   Writing, art, design, coaching, food, performance—creative ideas aren't hobbies, they're assets that can be built into income streams.

4. **Technology Levels the Field**
   From online platforms to self-publishing and social media, the tools for sharing and monetizing creative work are more accessible than ever.

5. **Prosperity Isn't Just Financial**
   Turning creativity into prosperity also means fulfillment, impact, and joy—the kind of wealth that money alone can't buy.

6. **It's Never Too Late**
   Women like Julia Child, Vera Wang, and Maggie Beer
   prove that 50+ is not a limitation, it's a launchpad.

♡ CLAIRE'S TIP

"Your creativity is not 'extra.' It's the engine. The moment you stop treating it like a side note and start treating it like your power source, prosperity follows."

PART THREE

Thriving Long-Term

11

From Paycheck to Power: Unlocking Financial Confidence After 50

For many women, money has been framed not as a tool for freedom, but as a source of fear. We're taught from a young age to be cautious with it, to save just in case, to avoid taking risks. We're praised for being frugal, for making do, for staying out of financial conversations altogether. The unspoken message? Let someone else, usually a man, handle it.

It's a narrative that's deeply ingrained. And it's one I, too, bought into.

In the early years of my business, I focused on what I did best: the creative side. I had vision, passion, and drive. My husband, also my business partner at the time, assured me he'd take care of the finances. I trusted him. I let him lead in that area, not because I wasn't capable, but because I'd been conditioned to believe it wasn't really my lane.

That decision came at a high cost.

When things started to unravel, I realized just how dangerous it can be to hand over financial control, even in a partnership built on trust. I was blindsided. Not because I wasn't smart, but because I had stepped back from something essential: financial awareness, financial power.

Looking back, I don't share this out of regret. I share it because too many women still find themselves in that same position—disconnected from their own money, their own power. And the truth is, that disconnect isn't just about numbers. It's about ownership. It's about being able to make decisions, set boundaries, and walk away when you need to.

Money, when understood and embraced, is not a burden. It's leverage. It's security. It's independence. And most importantly, it's **yours**.

Today, I understand that financial confidence isn't just about managing bills or preparing for retirement; it's about claiming independence, building security, and designing a future that reflects your values. The qualities of wisdom, resilience, and perspective that abound in women over 50, when paired with financial confidence, create freedom: the freedom to say no, to reinvent, to take risks, and to invest in yourself.

Financial empowerment after 50 isn't about becoming an overnight stock expert; it's about reframing money as a tool for choice, courage, and control.

Money conversations always made me feel uncomfortable, but with practice, I eventually overcame my reluctance. This is especially true for women who were raised to believe that asking for more is 'pushy' or 'ungrateful.'

Yet financial confidence is one of the most important skills you can develop at this stage of life. Whether you're re-entering the workforce, negotiating a new role, consulting, or launching a side hustle, knowing your value and asking for it changes everything.

Why Financial Confidence Matters

It's not just about money. Being fairly paid is about respect, recognition, and self-worth. You also set the tone. If you undervalue yourself, others will too.

It impacts your future, like it did mine. Every negotiation compounds over time, affecting savings, retirement, and lifestyle options.

No More Hoping. Start Asking: The Bold Art of Getting Paid What You're Worth

For years, you've shown up early, stayed late, solved problems no one else wanted, and kept the wheels turning. You're not just doing your job; you're doing it *well*. Yet when it comes time to talk salary, you hesitate. You downplay. You settle.

It's time to stop hoping someone will notice your value and start naming it. Salary negotiation isn't about being pushy or greedy. It's about recognizing your worth and having the courage to claim it. Because the truth is: you don't get what you deserve, you get what you ask for.

Know Your Value—Don't Wing It

Confidence in negotiation starts with clarity. You can't walk into that conversation hoping to be 'fair.' Remember what M. Scott Peck taught: *"Life is difficult."*

You need to come prepared with data, results, and receipts.

- Know the market rate for your role in your industry and region
- Keep a running list of your accomplishments, impact, and wins
- Quantify results wherever possible (revenue, savings, growth, efficiency)

This isn't bragging, it's evidence. You're not just asking for a number. You're making a case for the value you bring.

Detach Your Worth from Their Reaction

You are not your salary. Your value doesn't go up or down based on someone else's budget, mood, or feedback.

Negotiation can be uncomfortable, especially for women who've been taught to avoid conflict or not "ask for too much." But you are not too much, you are asking for what reflects your contribution.

Their discomfort is not your cue to shrink. It's a signal that you're showing up differently, and that's a good thing.

Don't Just Ask for More. Ask for Alignment

Sometimes, salary isn't the only negotiation point. Think holistically:

- More Personal Time Off (PTO)
- Flexible work schedule
- Professional development support
- A performance review sooner than the standard 12 months

Ask yourself: "What kind of compensation structure supports the life I want to live?" Then ask for it with clarity and calm.

Silence Is a Secret Weapon

Here's one of the most powerful tactics in salary negotiation: say your number, then stop talking. Don't fill the space. Don't apologize. Don't explain yourself into a corner.

Silence shows confidence. It invites them to respond, rather than putting you on the defensive. Practice saying your asking price, then waiting. You'll be amazed at how much power is in the pause.

Salary Negotiation Checklist

- **Audit your accomplishments**: Make a list of key achievements, projects, and results over the past 12–24 months.

- **Quantify your impact**: Highlight metrics: revenue generated, processes improved, costs saved, teams led.

- **Update your skills list**: Show how your experience is *current*, not outdated: include tech, leadership, and certifications.

- **Research market data**: Use salary tools (Glassdoor, PayScale, LinkedIn) to understand your role's value in your region and industry.

- **Know your minimum acceptable offer**: Have a clear number (or range) that reflects your worth, not just what you think they'll give.

Mindset Reset: Step Into Confidence

- **Drop the apology**: You're not 'lucky to be here,' you've earned your seat through experience and results.

- **Reframe your age as an asset**: You bring decades of leadership, emotional intelligence, and insight.

- **Practice your pitch aloud**: Rehearse asking for your salary clearly and confidently, without shrinking or justifying.

- **Visualize the conversation**: See yourself negotiating calmly, assertively, and without fear.

- **Remind yourself: This is business, not personal.** You're not asking for a favor, you're negotiating value.

During the Conversation: Be Direct, Then Pause

- **State your number or range with clarity**: "Based on my experience and the market, I'm looking for something in the $________ range."

- **Speak slowly, then pause**: Don't rush. Don't fill the silence. Let them respond.

- **Be ready to counter**: If their offer is low, say: *"I was expecting something closer to [your number], given the scope and my experience."*

- **Negotiate the full package**: Consider PTO, flex time, health benefits, bonus structure, professional development, and title.

- **Ask for time if needed**: You can say, *"Let me review this and get back to you tomorrow."*

After the Conversation: Own the Outcome

- **Get everything in writing**: Whether it's salary, benefits, or a review schedule, lock it down.

- **Plan your next value check-in**: Schedule a 6 or 12-month self-review to prepare for your next raise or role.

- **Celebrate the ask, even if it was a no**: Just having the conversation builds courage for the next one.

You're Not Charging for Your Time. You're Charging for Your *Power*

You've built a career, earned the experience, mastered your skills, and now you're stepping into consulting or freelance work. But when it comes to pricing, you hesitate.

You wonder, "Is this too much? Will they pay me? Am I really worth that number?"

Here's the truth: you're not just selling hours—you're selling decades of insight, intuition, and mastery. And yes, that's worth real money.

Stop Charging Like You're Just Getting Started

Many women underprice their services due to a fear of losing clients, being perceived as 'too expensive,' or taking up too much space. But your rate is a reflection of your value, not your need to be liked. As we have discussed in earlier chapters, you're not in the beginner seat. You're not 'just figuring it out.' You've been solving problems longer than most people have been in the industry.

Your experience shortens other people's learning curve, and that's priceless.

Simple Framework: How to Choose Your Rate with Confidence

- **Research your market:** What are others charging in your industry and niche? Look at experience level, location, and specialization.

- **Set a baseline rate:** Start with your desired monthly income and reverse-engineer the math. Don't forget taxes, tools, and downtime.

- **Decide your model:** Hourly, project-based, or retainer? (Hint: Hourly punishes efficiency. Project or value-based pricing often works better for experienced consultants.)

- **Practice saying it out loud:** "My rate for this engagement is $________" Then stop. Don't explain. Let it land.

If someone says, "That's too expensive," that doesn't mean your price is wrong. It means they're not your client.

You don't want bargain hunters. You want people who value quality, experience, and results. Your pricing is a signal. Let it speak clearly.

You've worked hard, gained experience, and built resilience over decades. That is worth something. Negotiating pay or setting consulting fees isn't about greed; it's about fairness and sustainability. By standing in your value, you also model confidence for the women who come after you.

For women over 50, career decisions aren't just about 'what's next,' they're also about *what's sustainable*. You're balancing your current work life with the bigger picture of financial security, freedom, and fulfillment in the years ahead.

Your Career Is the Runway, Retirement Is the Flight: Why You Can't Plan One Without the Other

Most people treat career and retirement as two separate conversations. First, you work. Then, one day, you retire. Simple, right?

Not exactly. I personally don't like the word retirement. Again, it was coined by men, for men, and like many things, it's been adapted for women. There is a huge industry built around fitting older people into a 'retirement' construct.

I have met many women who have been advised by male financial planners to sell their homes and move into a retirement village. While I believe that this is probably a positive long-term option, it's not something that women want to consider before the age of 70.

Did you know that the highest matched synonyms for the word 'retirement' are? Separation and Withdrawal. Women certainly don't want that.

However, I will use it here for the sake of comprehension. But I would like you to consider reframing the term retirement into your own personal meaning.

Your career and the decision to stop working are two ends of the same spectrum. Every decision you make about your career, your earnings, your benefits, your savings habits, even your work-life balance, directly shapes that end decision.

So, career planning over 50 needs to consider that this may be the case at whatever date you choose.

Earnings Today Shape Freedom Tomorrow: Your salary isn't just paying today's bills; it's funding your future independence. Each raise, each bonus, each promotion increases your ability to save and invest. But here's the catch: unless you're intentional, that money disappears into lifestyle creep.

When you connect career growth with retirement goals, you start asking different questions: How much of this increase can I funnel into my future self? How will this job decision impact my financial freedom later?

The payoff isn't just money, it's choice. More freedom to retire earlier, travel, volunteer, or pursue passions without financial stress.

Benefits Are More Than Perks: Healthcare, Superannuation, stock options aren't just job extras. They're building blocks for retirement security. Women, especially, can lose ground if they leave jobs without maximizing these benefits or if caregiving breaks stall contributions.

That's why career decisions shouldn't be weighed only by salary. A job with strong retirement benefits could be more valuable than one with a slightly bigger paycheck but no long-term support.

Your Career Timeline Shapes Your Retirement Timeline
Not everyone retires at 65. Some people work longer because they love their job. I do. Others leave early by choice—or by force. Health issues, caregiving responsibilities, or layoffs can shift the plan overnight.

Career planning with retirement in mind means building flexibility. Maybe that means exploring consulting or part-time work later, building a skill set that travels well, or creating multiple income streams. The stronger your career plan, the more adaptable your retirement plan can be.

Purpose Doesn't Retire Too often, women focus only on the financial side of retirement. But purpose matters just as much. If your career has been central to your identity, stepping away without a plan can feel disorienting.

Thinking ahead about what retirement *means*, volunteering, mentoring, starting a passion project, ensures you don't just prepare financially, but emotionally too. A fulfilling retirement starts with clarity, not coincidence.

Exercise: Practical Steps to Align Career and Retirement

- **Check your superannuation, pension, or retirement accounts.** Know what you have, what you're on track for, and where the gaps are.

- **Maximize earnings now.** Salary negotiations, consulting rates, and side hustles can significantly boost your financial base.

- **Diversify income streams.** Explore rental income, investments, or low-risk side businesses that can continue post-retirement.

- **Upskill with purpose.** Learn skills that can keep you relevant in flexible roles (e.g., digital literacy, coaching, mentoring).

- **Plan transitions.** Instead of stopping work abruptly, consider phased retirement, moving from full-time to part-time, or from employment to consulting.

Mindset Shifts That Help

Think 'options,' not 'end dates.' Retirement is a stage, not a switch.
Redefine work. Paid work, passion projects, and volunteering can all play a role.
View money as freedom. The more intentional your financial planning, the more freedom you'll have in deciding *how* you spend your time.

Retirement doesn't mean the end of your contribution. By weaving retirement planning into your career strategy now, you're building not just financial security, but peace of mind and choice.

Retirement and Career Planning Checklist

Career Planning

- **Update your skills**: Stay current with industry trends, certifications, and technology to protect employability.
- **Evaluate your career path**: Are you in a role you want to continue, or is it time to pivot into consulting, part-time, or passion work?
- **Build your network**: At this stage, relationships matter more than résumés. Keep connections alive.
- **Negotiate strategically**: Ask for raises, bonuses, or benefits that directly boost your retirement savings.

- **Explore flexible options**: Identify work you could scale back to later, instead of fully retiring overnight.

Financial Foundations

- **Know your number**: Estimate how much you'll need in retirement (consider healthcare, housing, lifestyle).
- **Max out contributions**: Take advantage of catch-up contributions in your retirement accounts.
- **Review employer benefits**: Look closely at pensions, stock options, or retirement matches you may be underutilizing.
- **Reduce debt**: Prioritize paying down high-interest debt before retirement.
- **Diversify income**: Consider side hustles, consulting, or investments that could create additional retirement streams.

Health & Wellness

- **Check healthcare coverage**: Understand what your employer, Medicare, or private insurance will (and won't) cover.
- **Prioritize preventive care**: Regular checkups, exercise, and stress management now save money and health later.

- **Protect energy at work**: Balance workload with caregiving or personal demands to prevent burnout before retirement.

Purpose & Lifestyle

- **Define your retirement vision**: What do you want your days to look like? Travel, volunteering, family, new projects?
- **Experiment now**: Test activities, hobbies, or part-time work while you're still employed.
- **Strengthen relationships**: Invest time in community and family ties that will matter post-career.
- **Mentor or share expertise**: Passing on knowledge creates meaning and legacy beyond your paycheck.

Action Steps

- Schedule a financial review with a trusted advisor.
- Update your CV/LinkedIn for future opportunities.
- Increase retirement contributions by even 1–2%.
- Choose one activity that aligns with your retirement vision and start it now.
- Set boundaries at work to preserve energy for both the present and future you.

⚝ Key Takeaways: From Paycheck to Power

- **Financial Confidence Is a Skill, Not a Personality Trait**
  You don't have to be a "numbers person" to manage money wisely. Confidence comes from clarity, education, and consistent action.

- **Your Paycheck Is a Tool. Not Your Only Source of Power**
  Income is just one piece. Investments, savings, side ventures, and even downsizing can build financial strength that goes beyond a monthly paycheck.

- **Retirement Isn't the End of Earning. It's the Start of Redefining**
  Work may shift, but income opportunities don't vanish. Consulting, part-time work, or passion projects can fuel both income and purpose.

- **Planning Protects Freedom**
  The more intentional you are with savings, healthcare, and debt management, the more choices you'll have in retirement. Planning equals power.

- **Mindset Matters as Much as Math**
  Fear and avoidance drain energy. Reframing money as a tool for security, freedom, and joy unlocks confidence and control.

- **It's Never Too Late to Rewrite Your Financial Story**
  Whether you're catching up on savings or ready to expand wealth, every step you take now compounds. Small, steady actions build a powerful future.

♀ CLAIRE'S TIP

"Money is not just about survival, it's about choice. The moment you stop fearing it and start directing it, you step into power. Your 50s and beyond aren't too late, they're the perfect time to claim control."

12

Own Your Time, Own Your Life: The New Rules of Work-Life Harmony

In early 2007 at 75, my mother Angela, was diagnosed with a serious condition and sadly passed three months later. At the time, I was managing a workforce of around 10 contractors and had five specialized newsletters and websites targeted to senior executives within the global consumer electronics industry.

As a result of my success with connectwomen website, I was also a global keynote speaker, presenting to international companies on how they can create a marketing to women culture.

My work had to be exact, relevant, and timely, not only for my subscribers and advertisers. I was also constantly challenged by print competitors who were slow to enter the digital space and were determined to see me fail.

Balancing caregiving, health, and work is no small feat. I believe it was the catalyst that demonstrated to my husband and business partner that I may not always be there putting him first.

It was a constant juggle, and most days, it felt like I was holding everything together with sheer willpower and caffeine. I also managed to garner hundreds of dollars in speeding fines as I often raced from my office to see my mother at Royal North Shore Hospital in Sydney.

If you have lived a full life, you will inevitably face these life crises sooner or later. You're showing up for others, staying afloat at work, trying to prioritize your health, and doing it all while pretending you're fine. But here's the truth: you can do a lot, yes. But you're not meant to carry it all without boundaries, support, or rest.

If you're in the thick of it, this isn't about doing *more.* It's about doing it *differently.*

You Can't Be Everything to Everyone—Every Day

Caregiving takes a toll. Whether you're caring for aging parents, children, a partner, or all three, it's emotional labor that's rarely visible but always exhausting. And when you're also holding down a job and trying to take care of your own health, burnout is right around the corner.

The first shift? Drop the guilt. You're not failing anyone by setting limits. In fact, boundaries make you *more effective,* not less. The people you care for need the best of you—not what's left of you.

Your Health Is Not Optional

This isn't the season to put yourself last. If you're skipping sleep, living off snacks, or running on empty, your body will eventually call time-out, whether you like it or not.

- You don't need a perfect routine. Start small:
- Block 20 minutes for movement.
- Prep one healthy meal a day.
- Get to bed 30 minutes earlier.
- Say no without a full explanation.

Protect your energy like its fuel, because it is. You can't pour from an empty tank, and you shouldn't try.

Work Is a Piece of Your Life—Not the Whole Thing

Your job may be demanding, but it doesn't own you. Too often, women in caregiving roles overcompensate at work, trying to prove they're still 'on top of it.' But real power comes from clarity and boundaries, not from being the last one online at night.

It's Okay to Ask for Help

You're strong, but that doesn't mean you should do everything alone. Whether it's asking siblings to step up, hiring a part-time caregiver, or delegating more at work, *let people help you.* Needing help is not a weakness. It's wisdom.

Support systems don't magically appear. They're built, brick by brick, conversation by conversation.

You Deserve to Thrive—Not Just Survive

You weren't meant to live in constant survival mode. Yes, there are seasons where life is heavy, but even in those seasons, you deserve moments of joy, rest, and lightness. Don't wait for the chaos to end to start living.

Start now. Even five minutes of breathing room is a powerful act of self-respect.

Fuel First: Why Your Health and Energy Aren't Extras. They're the Engine

You can have the best intentions, the longest to-do list, the biggest heart, but without energy, nothing moves.

The truth is: your health and energy aren't luxuries. They're *non-negotiables*. Yet they're often the first things sacrificed when life gets busy, stressful, or demanding. You push your needs aside, tell yourself you'll rest later, and keep showing up for everyone else, until your body says, *enough*.

Here's the real talk: if your energy is gone, everything else slows down with it. Prioritizing your health isn't self-indulgence. It's self-leadership.

You don't just need time—you need the energy to *use* that time well. Health is what makes focus possible. It's what gives your mood stability, your mind clarity, and your body the stamina to follow through on what matters most.

When you treat your energy like currency, you stop wasting it on things that drain you. That includes overcommitting, toxic relationships, skipping meals, and ignoring sleep.

Ask yourself every morning: *"Where's my energy going today—and is it worth it?"*

Your Health Is Not a Side Project

Too often, women put their health on the "when I have time" shelf. But your health is not a background task. It's the foundation. What does prioritizing it look like? Not perfection. Not rigid rules. Just consistent, sustainable choices that add up:

- Drinking more water than caffeine.
- Walking instead of sitting all day.
- Cooking a basic meal instead of skipping food.
- Saying no to preserve energy instead of pleasing by default.
- Start where you are. You don't need a 90-day plan. You need a 9-minute commitment, daily.

You Can't Power Through Forever

Your body keeps score. If you're constantly tired, moody, wired but exhausted, or getting sick more often, it's not in your head. It's in your nervous system, your hormones, your gut, your sleep cycle. That's your body waving a red flag.

Pushing through is a short-term tactic with long-term costs. *Listening* is the better strategy. When you prioritize rest, nourishment, movement, and boundaries—you don't just feel better. You make better decisions, show up more fully, and recover faster when life hits hard.

Energy Management Is the New Time Management

You can schedule your day to the minute, but if you're running on fumes, you won't get far. Instead of asking, "How do I fit more in?", ask: "What fuels me—and what drains me?"

- What tasks give you energy?
- Who do you feel better around?
- What habits make your body feel stronger?

Make more space for those things. Cut the rest without guilt.

Designing Work Around Life (Not the Other Way Around)

The advantage of experience is knowing that careers can be shaped, not just endured. At this stage, it's worth exploring models of work that allow for flexibility: consulting, part-time roles, portfolio careers, or phased retirement, as we have detailed in earlier chapters. The key is to align work with your values and responsibilities.

Time-blocking: Plan caregiving, health, and work in your calendar to reduce constant overlap.

Boundary setting: Protect non-work hours for recovery and relationships.

Leveraging technology: Use online tools for remote collaboration, appointment scheduling, or even virtual caregiving check-ins.

You can power through a deadline. You can ignore exhaustion. You can even fake a smile. But when your emotions are out of sync, everything starts to feel off.

Emotional harmony isn't about being happy all the time. It's about being *honest* with yourself, allowing space for your full range of feelings without letting any single one take the wheel.

When you cultivate emotional harmony, you stop reacting from chaos and start responding from clarity. You make decisions from a grounded place, not a triggered one. You stop swinging between extremes and find your center again.

Here's how you start.

Stop Policing Your Emotions

One of the fastest ways to stay stuck emotionally is to judge what you're feeling. You tell yourself you "shouldn't" be angry, or "should" be grateful, or that sadness is weak.

But emotions are messengers, not moral statements.

Anger might be telling you something needs to change. Sadness may signal a need for rest or release. Anxiety could be pointing to something unresolved.

When you stop fighting your feelings and start listening to them, the intensity begins to dissolve. You create space for integration instead of suppression.

Build Emotional Check-Ins into Your Day

Most people wait until they're emotionally overwhelmed to pause. But by then, it's already a fire drill.

Emotional harmony comes from *daily maintenance,* not damage control.

Try this: three times a day, stop and ask:

- What am I feeling?
- What triggered this?
- What do I need right now?

This simple practice builds self-awareness like a muscle. You start catching emotional shifts earlier and recovering faster.

Detach From Drama, Not Emotion

Cultivating emotional harmony doesn't mean numbing out or rising above your feelings. It means creating enough inner space to *feel without spiraling.*

You can feel sad without becoming despair.

You can feel angry without becoming destructive.

You can feel anxious without losing control.

This takes practice, but it starts with one shift: *observe, don't absorb.*

You are not your feelings. You are the one *experiencing* them. That separation is your power.

Maya, 53 – Creative Consultant & Caregiver

Challenge: Maya is a seasoned graphic designer running her own freelance business. When her mother was diagnosed with early-stage Alzheimer's, Maya stepped in as the primary caregiver. Within months, she was overwhelmed, juggling client deadlines, emotional strain, and nonstop caregiving with no downtime.

Shift: Maya hit a breaking point when she missed an important client meeting due to exhaustion. That day, she gave herself permission to stop being the sole support system. She hired a part-time caregiver (just 10 hours a week) and began blocking two hours every morning for her own work—no interruptions, no guilt.

Now: Maya's learned to separate her days into clear "zones"—mornings for work, afternoons for caregiving, evenings for rest. Her business hasn't suffered—in fact, it's more focused. She feels less reactive and more present. "I don't do more," she says, "I just do what matters, when it matters."

Lisa, 57 – Executive Leader, Empty Nester, Wellness Advocate

Challenge: Lisa spent most of her adult life building her career in tech while raising two kids. After they moved out, she was left with a full-time executive role and a deep feeling of emptiness. Her calendar was packed, but her life felt hollow.

Shift: Lisa realized she had mastered productivity but neglected joy. She scaled her workweek down to four longer days, negotiated one work-from-home day per week, and committed to three personal "non-negotiables": morning movement, 30 minutes of solo reflection, and a weekly dinner with friends.

Now: Lisa leads her team with more creativity and less stress. She's also training for her first 10K, writing a blog on leadership and wellness, and finally reading for pleasure again. "Work-life harmony isn't about balance," she says, "It's about rhythm. And I finally found mine."

Denise, 61 – Former Teacher Turned Coach

Challenge: After 30 years of teaching, Denise retired—and found herself totally unmoored. The structure, identity, and purpose she had built her life around vanished overnight. She threw herself into volunteering and family support, but burnout crept in fast.

Shift: A simple journaling prompt changed everything: *What do I want this chapter of my life to feel like?* Denise realized she was still operating on obligation, not desire. She got certified as a life coach and began working part-time with women in midlife transitions.

Now: Denise coaches 12 hours a week, teaches a local yoga class, and spends slow mornings walking in nature. Her life is no longer measured by output but by alignment. "I used to live by the bell," she laughs. "Now I live by my values."

What These Women Have in Common:

They stopped chasing 'balance' and started building *alignment.* They replaced guilt with boundaries and busywork with intentionality. They didn't wait for permission to change their lives—they gave it to themselves.

Protect Your Emotional Energy Like It's Gold

You don't owe everyone access to your inner world. You don't have to explain yourself to people who don't feel safe. You don't have to attend every emotional invitation someone throws your way.

Protecting your peace might look like:

- Saying "I need space to think about this."
- Not responding right away.
- Leaving the room when energy feels chaotic.
- Boundaries aren't just physical; they're emotional filters, too.

Exercise: Create Your Harmony Map

On a sheet of paper, draw three overlapping circles labeled Work, Caregiving, and Health.

In each circle, list the top three priorities you have right now. Where the circles overlap, note areas of tension or conflict (for example, "Work deadlines clash with medical appointments").

Then, brainstorm one practical step you can take to reduce conflict in each overlap zone—such as asking for flexible hours, booking a caregiver backup, or scheduling exercise into your lunch break.

Keep this map visible to remind you that harmony is an ongoing practice, not a final destination.

✦ Key Takeaways: Work-Life Harmony

1. **Work-Life Harmony Is Personal, Not Perfect**
   It's not about balancing everything equally, it's about creating a rhythm that fits your life, values, and energy.

2. **Boundaries Create Space for What Matters**
   Saying "no" to what drains you makes room for what fuels you. Harmony starts with protecting your time and emotional bandwidth.

3. **Harmony Shifts with Life Stages**
   Whether you're caregiving, changing careers, or entering a new phase, what harmony looks like will change—and that's normal. Adapt as you evolve.

4. **Alignment > Hustle**
   The goal isn't to do more, it's to do what *matters more.* Focus beats busyness every time.

5. **Support Isn't a Luxury—It's a Strategy**
   Delegating, asking for help, or outsourcing isn't a weakness. It's how smart, resilient women sustain their energy and purpose.

6. **Joy and Recovery Are Non-Negotiable**
   Harmony includes rest, fun, and fulfillment. If you're not nourishing yourself, you're just surviving—not thriving.

💡 CLAIRE'S TIP

"Work-life harmony isn't found, it's *designed*. Stop waiting for balance to happen. Start choosing what stays, what goes, and what lights you up. You're the architect of your life. Not the assistant to everyone else's."

13

The Power of No: How Setting Boundaries Saves Your Energy, Sanity, and Soul

For decades, many women have been conditioned to say *yes*—to help, to smooth things over, to keep the peace. Whether it was for family, career, or community, the instinct to accommodate others often came at the expense of their own needs. But by the time you hit 50, something shifts. You've seen enough, done enough, and *felt enough* to know: your time, energy, and peace are not limitless.

And this is exactly why women over 50 need boundaries. Not just to protect themselves, but to finally *honor themselves.*

1. You've Earned the Right to Choose What Matters

At this stage of life, you are no longer proving yourself to anyone. You've already built careers, raised children, navigated relationships, and weathered more than a few storms. You carry wisdom. You've paid your dues.

Setting boundaries isn't selfish—it's earned.

Boundaries reflect your values and protect your time from being hijacked by guilt or obligation. You are allowed to say *no* without explanation. You are allowed to change your mind. You are allowed to walk away from what drains you and lean into what restores you.

This is your season of selective energy. You get to choose what gets your "yes."

2. Unspoken Expectations Are a Silent Killer

One of the biggest causes of burnout among women over 50 is the weight of *invisible labor*. You're expected to remember birthdays, manage family logistics, stay connected to everyone, host holidays, help aging parents, and support grown children—all without complaint.

Much of this pressure comes from unspoken expectations, others assume you'll take care of things, and you've silently agreed, often out of habit or duty.

Boundaries make those expectations visible. They clarify roles, reduce resentment, and stop the slow emotional leak that happens when you're stretched too thin but afraid to speak up.

Clear boundaries don't ruin relationships—they clarify them.

3. You Can't Be Everything to Everyone (And You Never Had to Be)

One of the most liberating truths for women over 50 is this: **You are not responsible for managing everyone's emotions.**

You can be kind without being a doormat. You can be helpful without being on call. You can be loving and still say, "This doesn't work for me."

Setting boundaries lets you step out of the caretaker trap and into a more honest, balanced way of being. It teaches others how to treat you, and more importantly, it teaches *you* to treat yourself with dignity.

4. Health and Energy Are Not Infinite Resources

Let's get real: your body changes after 50. Hormonal shifts, stress, sleep, and energy levels all demand more attention. If you continue to overextend, the cost won't just be emotional—it'll be physical.

Chronic stress, inflammation, fatigue, and burnout are serious risks when boundaries are weak.

Every time you say yes to something that drains you, you're borrowing energy from something that matters more—your health, your creativity, your peace of mind.

Boundaries are a form of health care. They're preventive medicine for your body, mind, and spirit.

5. Your Relationships Will Improve (Even If They Get Uncomfortable First)

Let's be honest, setting boundaries might rock the boat. People who've benefited from your over-giving may not be thrilled when you stop. But that discomfort is part of the process.

You are not responsible for their reaction.

Healthy relationships will adjust. The ones that don't? Maybe they weren't as healthy as you thought.

When you set clear boundaries, your relationships become more honest. You're not hiding your needs. You're not pretending everything is okay when it's not. That honesty creates deeper respect, even if it comes with growing pains.

6. Boundaries Make Room for Joy

When you stop filling your calendar with obligations, you start filling your life with *choice*.

Boundaries create space—for rest, for hobbies, for laughter, and for things that bring you joy. They help you reconnect to who you are *outside* of who you've been for everyone else.

Many women over 50 find themselves wondering, "Who am I now?" The answer often lies where your boundaries begin, where you reclaim your time, attention, and self-worth.

Joy doesn't require more effort. It requires more room. And boundaries make that room.

7. It's Never Too Late to Start

If you've spent many years people-pleasing, it can feel unnatural, even scary, to start saying no. But it's never too late to draw the line and change the rules.

You can start small:

- Block time for yourself every day.
- Say no to things that don't feel right.
- Don't explain or justify your decisions.
- Practice silence after you say no.

It will feel awkward at first. That's okay. It's not about perfection, it's about progress.

Every time you hold a boundary, you build trust in yourself. You prove that your well-being matters. And that changes everything.

Why Boundaries Matter More Now

At this stage of life, time and energy are your most precious resources. Unlike in earlier career phases, the goal is not to prove yourself endlessly but to protect your well-being while still contributing meaningfully. Boundaries are the invisible lines that preserve your mental, physical, and emotional health.

- **Without boundaries**: Overcommitment, guilt, exhaustion, resentment.
- **With boundaries**: Clarity, focus, energy, and healthier relationships.

When the Fire Becomes Smoke: How to Spot Burnout Before It Consumes You

Burnout doesn't start with collapse. It starts quietly.

You feel a little more tired than usual. A little more irritable. A little more checked out. You brush it off, push through, tell yourself everyone's tired. You keep going.

Until one day, something gives.

And that's the thing about burnout: it doesn't knock. It leaks.

Burnout Is Not Just Stress

Let's get something clear, burnout isn't about being "busy." It's about being disconnected.

It's the slow erosion of joy, motivation, and energy. It's waking up and dreading the day for no specific reason. It's doing everything you're supposed to be doing and still feeling like you're drowning. It's a cycle of emotional depletion that can wreck your body, mind, and sense of self.

And it's more common than most people admit.

Whether you're juggling a career, caregiving, relationships, or just trying to hold it all together—burnout doesn't discriminate. But it *does* leave clues.

The Early Warning Signs You Shouldn't Ignore

Burnout sneaks in. Here's what it often looks like before it fully hits:

- You're constantly tired, even after a full night's sleep
- Your patience is thin, and small things feel huge
- You feel detached from your work or your purpose
- Your motivation has flatlined
- You're more cynical, snappy, or numb than usual
- Everything feels like an obligation, even fun things
- You fantasize about quitting, running away, or hiding

These signs aren't just bad moods. They're your body and mind saying: *"This isn't sustainable."*

The earlier you listen, the easier it is to course-correct.

Burnout Loves High Performers

Ironically, the people most likely to burn out are the ones who *care the most*.

You work hard. You show up. You take pride in doing things well. But that same drive, if left unchecked, can become a trap.

When you never rest, never say no, and never ask for help, you're setting yourself up for collapse. And high performers often miss the signs because they normalize over-functioning.

But just because you can handle it doesn't mean you should.

The Cultural Lie: Keep Pushing

We live in a culture that glorifies hustle and labels rest as lazy. That mindset is a fast track to burnout.

Here's the truth: **you are not a machine.** You are not designed to operate at full capacity, every hour of the day, forever. You need cycles. You need downtime. You need boundaries.

Rest is not a reward. It's a requirement.

And avoiding burnout is not a weakness: it's strategy.

Avoiding Burnout Starts with One Word: *Enough*

At the core of burnout is the fear that you're not doing enough. That if you stop, things will fall apart. That people will be disappointed. That you'll lose your edge.

But what if *enough* became your power word?

Enough sleep. Enough space. Enough "no" to protect your "yes."

Living from a place of *enough* doesn't mean settling—it means setting a pace that honors your well-being over the illusion of perfection.

Strategies to Avoid Burnout (Before It's Too Late)

1. Get Honest About Your Capacity

You're not who you were at 25. And that's a good thing. Your energy, priorities, and limits evolve. Stop pretending you can do it all, all the time. Start asking, "What do I actually have the bandwidth for?"

2. Set Boundaries Without Guilt

Burnout thrives in environments where "no" feels forbidden. Your time is yours. Your inbox is not your emergency room. Your weekends are not free labor.

3. Unplug Like You Mean It

Technology never stops and neither will you if you don't take control. Create hard stops in your day. Phone down. Laptop closed. The world paused. Your nervous system needs actual off time to reset.

4. Redefine Productivity

More doesn't always mean better. Productivity isn't how much you do—it's how much you do *well* and *with purpose.* Learn to measure your day not by how busy you were, but by how aligned you felt.

5. Reclaim Joy—Intentionally

Burnout strips life of color. Fight back by injecting moments of light. Read for pleasure. Move your body in ways that feel good. Laugh. Take the long route home. Schedule joy the same way you schedule meetings.

6. Get Support Without Waiting for a Breakdown

You don't have to hit rock bottom to ask for help. Therapy, coaching, or simply talking to someone who gets it can make a massive difference. You don't have to carry it all alone. You never did.

7. Listen to Your Body—It Speaks First

Before burnout hits your life, it hits your body. Pay attention. Headaches, tight chest, foggy thinking, stomach issues—these aren't random. They're signals. Your body whispers before it screams.

Burnout Self-Check: Are You Running on Empty?

Use this quick checklist to see if burnout may be creeping in. Check all that apply:

- I feel exhausted even after a full night's sleep
- I'm more irritable or impatient than usual
- I feel emotionally numb or detached
- I'm losing interest in things I used to enjoy
- I fantasize about quitting, disappearing, or starting over
- I find it hard to focus or make decisions
- I feel guilty when I rest or take time for myself
- I say yes when I really want to say no
- I've stopped taking care of my body (sleep, food, movement)
- I feel like I'm just going through the motions

If you checked 3 or more: You're likely in the burnout zone. **If you checked 5 or more:** It's time to take action now—not later.

Burnout Doesn't Mean You're Broken

If you're burned out or on the edge of it, it's not because you're weak. It's because you're human. You've been over-giving, over-performing, and under-recovering. That's not a flaw. That's a pattern. And patterns can change.

Burnout isn't your identity. It's a message. And that message is: you need care. Not criticism. Not caffeine. Not a productivity hack. Care.

Avoiding burnout isn't about slowing down forever. It's about finding a rhythm that lets you move through life without losing yourself in the process.

Because when your fire is steady, not frantic, you burn brighter, longer and more powerfully than ever before.

You deserve that kind of light.

✨ Key Takeaways: Boundaries Are the Framework of Freedom

Saying "Yes" to Everything Is a Fast Track to Burnout
Overcommitting leads to depletion. Every time you say yes out of guilt or fear, you're borrowing energy from your future self.

Boundaries Are Not Barriers—They're Filters
Boundaries don't push people away; they protect your energy and prioritize what truly matters. They teach others how to treat you and teach *you* to value your own time.

1. **Burnout Isn't Just Exhaustion—It's Emotional Disconnection**

   It's not about being busy. It's about being numb, joyless, and running on autopilot. That's your cue to slow down, not speed up.

2. **If You Don't Define Your Limits, Someone Else Will**

   Whether it's work, family, or friends, people will take as much as you allow. Boundaries are how you stop being everyone's backup plan and start being your own priority.

3. **Recovery Is Not a Luxury—It's a Lifeline**

   Rest, stillness, and space aren't indulgent—they're essential. Burnout isn't cured by a weekend off; it requires rethinking your pace and protecting your peace.

4. **Protecting Your Peace Is a Daily Practice**

   Avoiding burnout isn't a one-time fix—it's a commitment to ongoing self-respect, honest check-ins, and boundaries that evolve as you do.

💡 CLAIRE'S TIP

"Stop asking, 'Can I handle more?' and start asking, 'What can I release?' Your life isn't meant to be a test of endurance. It's meant to be *lived*. Protect your spark before it burns out. You don't owe anyone your depletion."

14

Ageless Relevance: The Art of Staying Resilient in a Changing World

The modern workplace is evolving at a faster pace than ever. Technology, flexible work models, and shifting industries mean that staying relevant isn't just about keeping up, but about continuously growing, adapting, and thriving.

One of the key assets that employers found attractive when, over 60 I was eventually able to start looking for a job, was my understanding and skills in using basic technology. I understood how to post on social media, how a website operated, and had updated my writing skills.

After 19 years of working as a media entrepreneur, and then retraining as a coach, I returned to the paid workforce at 60 and was continually offered senior editorial and social media roles. I worked in these roles until I had rebuilt my financial foundation and decided to focus on coaching women to success at 67.

One of the other aspects that enabled me, a woman clearly over 50, to be included on the interview list, was my personal stability. Despite all the difficulties that I had faced, I had a clear track record of successfully finishing projects, and my references spoke strongly to that.

One of the affirmations that I used to ensure that I completed every project I undertook was, *"I successfully complete everything that I begin."*

This slowly built my confidence, which began to show up in job interviews. One thing I learned is that employers in any profession value confidence and positivity, because they know that you will bring these qualities to their enterprise.

I had also faced down the bogey of ageism and went into interviews believing that I was one of the best candidates for the role.

Ageism exists, and we can't change it unless we show up as successful, confident older women. I believe that for women over 50, resilience and a growth mindset are the twin engines that power both confidence and opportunity.

Redefining Relevance: Why Your Voice Matters More Than Ever

Relevance is often treated like a fleeting commodity, something reserved for the young, the trendy, the new. But for women over 50, relevance isn't about chasing what's fashionable; it's about owning what's timeless.

I still value and use my grandmother's and mother's beautiful English china. In a disposable age, I know that these items were made to last.

Just like fine classic china, your depth of knowledge, resilience, and lived experience are not anchors holding you back—they are the very qualities that make you indispensable.

To redefine relevance is to reclaim authority over how the world perceives you. It's about shifting from asking, "Am I still relevant?" to declaring, "Here is the value I bring." And that declaration grows more powerful, not less, with age.

Cultural narratives often suggest that relevance comes from youth, novelty, or speed. But when you redefine relevance, you move away from external validation and toward self-defined impact. Relevance becomes measured not in likes or trends, but in the lives you touch, the problems you solve, and the wisdom you share.

Relevance as Legacy

Your relevance is also not tied to a single role or career. It is woven through every pivot, every reinvention, every moment of courage. For some women, this might mean starting a consultancy that applies decades of expertise. For others, it may be mentoring younger professionals, writing a book, or championing causes that matter deeply. The common thread? Relevance grounded in purpose, not performance.

Take Iris Apfel, who became a global fashion icon in her 90s—not because she chased trends, but because she embodied authenticity. Or Maya Angelou, whose later works continue to shape culture long after her passing. These women prove that relevance expands with age, provided you choose to step forward rather than fade back.

Practical Ways to Redefine Relevance

- **Audit Your Impact:** List the spaces where your voice still makes a difference. Your workplace, community, family, or creative endeavors.

- **Stay Curious:** Relevance thrives on curiosity. Read widely, engage with new technology, and remain open to learning.

- **Share Generously:** Write, speak, mentor, and create. Every contribution is a ripple that extends your influence.

- **Anchor in Purpose:** Define relevance on your own terms. What matters to you most right now—and how can you shape your world around it?

Unlocking What's Next: The Power of a Growth Mindset After 50

When we hear the phrase "growth mindset," it often brings to mind schoolchildren or young professionals eager to learn.

But the truth is, this concept becomes even more powerful later in life. At 50 and beyond, many women feel society's whisper that they've already peaked. A growth mindset silences that whisper and replaces it with a louder, bolder truth: *you are still becoming.*

Coined by psychologist Carol Dweck, a *growth mindset* is the belief that your abilities, intelligence, and talents can be developed through effort, learning, and persistence. It's the opposite of a fixed mindset, which says you've either "got it" or you don't. After 50, adopting a growth mindset can be the difference between stagnation and transformation.

Why? Because the world doesn't stop changing, and neither should you.

The myth that learning slows down or stops as we age is just that. A myth. The brain remains adaptable. Neuroplasticity, the brain's ability to form new connections, doesn't expire. But to tap into it, you have to challenge yourself, stay curious, and stay willing to stretch beyond your comfort zone.

A growth mindset keeps you in motion. It invites you to take risks, try new things, and reinvent parts of your life that no longer serve you. That might mean switching careers, going back to school, starting a business, learning a new skill, or simply shifting the way you see yourself.

If you are asking, "What now?" The answer starts with reframing the question. Instead of "What am I still able to do?" try "What do I want to do next—and what will it take to get there?"

That simple shift opens up possibilities. It changes your self-talk from limiting to empowering. You stop seeing age as a boundary and start using it as a base of experience, wisdom, and strength.

Of course, doubt creeps in. That's natural. But a growth mindset doesn't deny fear, it works with it. It asks, "What can I learn from this?" "What's the opportunity here? How can I improve?"

You don't need to overhaul your life overnight. Small steps compound. Read more. Ask questions. Challenge your assumptions. Say yes to the thing that scares you a little.

Unlocking what's next isn't about chasing a finish line—it's about staying in the race with eyes wide open. With a growth mindset, life after 50 isn't about slowing down. It's about leveling up.

- **Reframe challenges as opportunities**: Each setback is a lesson.
- **Celebrate progress, not perfection**: Small wins build momentum.
- **Replace "I can't" with "I can't yet."**

Practical Ways to Stay Current

- **Learn continuously**: Take online courses, attend workshops, or join webinars. Even short learning bursts keep your skills fresh.

- **Mentor and reverse-mentor**: Share your expertise while learning from younger colleagues about technology or cultural trends.

- **Network with purpose**: Surround yourself with people who challenge and inspire you.

- **Read widely**: Industry news, podcasts, and books expand your perspective beyond daily routines.

Resilience in Action: Turning Setbacks into Stepping Stones

Resilience isn't just the ability to survive difficulty; it's the art of transforming adversity into growth. For women over 50, resilience is often forged in the crucible of lived experience—navigating career changes, financial challenges, caregiving responsibilities, health hurdles, and sometimes the quiet invisibility that society projects onto older women. Far from being a weakness, these lived realities become the raw material for strength, adaptability, and renewal.

Resilience is not about 'toughing it out' or denying hardship. Instead, it's about acknowledging challenges, processing them, and choosing to rise again, this time wiser and more resourceful. Psychologists describe it as the ability to "bounce forward," not just back. Each trial leaves behind insight and courage, shaping a more powerful self.

Everyday Acts of Resilience

Resilience often shows up in small, everyday ways:

- Pivoting careers after redundancy and turning skills into a consultancy.
- Returning to study in your 50s or 60s to step into a new field.
- Managing caregiving duties while still pursuing professional ambitions.
- Rebuilding financially after divorce or loss, refusing to let circumstances dictate destiny.

These actions, though sometimes quiet and unseen, represent resilience in motion—courage harnessed into practical steps.

Women Who Inspire

Consider Dame Judi Dench, who wasn't widely known outside Britain until her 60s and went on to win an Academy Award at 64.

Or Harriet Thompson, who ran her first marathon at 76 and went on to become the oldest woman to complete a marathon at 92. Their achievements weren't about ignoring age or obstacles, but about redefining what's possible through determination and grit.

Closer to home, many women you meet every day are embodying resilience, those who reinvent their careers after job loss, who start small businesses after retirement, or who step into caregiving roles while still protecting their dreams. Their resilience lies not in avoiding hardship but in continually finding new ways to thrive.

Case Study: Quentin Bryce — A Trailblazer in Leadership and Resilience

When Quentin Bryce was sworn in as Australia's first female Governor-General in 2008, she was 65, and more than a personal achievement, it was a landmark moment for women across the nation. Her appointment signaled that women not only belonged in the highest offices of public life but could embody them with grace, strength, and vision.

Bryce's story is one of resilience, persistence, and a deep commitment to social progress. Born in 1942 in Brisbane, she grew up in a small country town in Queensland. At a time when women's career options were limited, she studied law at the University of Queensland, becoming one of the first women admitted to the Queensland Bar in 1965. From the beginning, she challenged norms simply by stepping into spaces traditionally reserved for men.

Her career was marked by a fierce dedication to human rights, equality, and education. She worked as a university lecturer, lawyer, and advocate for women and children. Bryce became the founding director of the Queensland Women's Information Service, and later held roles as Federal Sex Discrimination

Commissioner and Governor of Queensland. Each of these milestones built her reputation as a leader who championed inclusivity and fairness.

When she assumed the office of Governor-General, Bryce spoke of her role as being one of "encouragement and inclusion", vowing to represent "all Australians". She was visible in communities large and small, offering support to marginalised groups and reminding women in particular that leadership was within their reach.

Bryce's journey also illustrates resilience in action. She navigated systemic gender barriers throughout her career and balanced public service with raising five children. Her ability to remain poised under scrutiny, to challenge outdated structures, and to continually push for equity shows that leadership after 50 is not only possible—it can be transformative.

For women today, Quentin Bryce stands as a role model: proof that persistence, vision, and resilience can dismantle barriers and reshape what leadership looks like in Australia.

Lessons from Quentin Bryce

- **Break Barriers by Showing Up**: Bryce didn't wait for permission, she stepped into male-dominated spaces and stayed the course until her presence reshaped expectations.

- **Lead with Inclusion**: Her commitment to representing all Australians shows that true leadership is about lifting others, not just advancing yourself.

- **Balance with Grace**: Raising five children while building a groundbreaking career, she modeled resilience through both ambition and care.

- **Redefine Success Later in Life**: Bryce's most visible role, Governor-General, came in her 60s, proving that your strongest chapter may still be ahead.

Building Your Own Resilience Toolkit

Resilience is not a fixed trait, it's a muscle that can be strengthened with practice. Some strategies include:

- Reframing challenges: Instead of asking, "Why me?" ask, "What can I learn from this?"

- Cultivating support: Lean on networks of women, friends, and mentors who remind you that you're not alone.
- Prioritizing health: Energy fuels resilience—sleep, nutrition, and movement are non-negotiables.
- Practicing gratitude: Focusing on what's working, even in dark seasons, creates emotional balance.
- Allowing flexibility: Resilience thrives when you let go of rigid expectations and remain open to new paths.

Why Resilience Matters Now

At this stage of life, as we have identified, women have many superpowers, and resilience is one of them. It is what enables you to step into reinvention, face down ageism, navigate uncertainty, and still claim joy, purpose, and impact. Resilience turns "setback stories" into "comeback stories," ensuring that no matter what life throws your way, you remain the author of your own narrative.

Cultivating the 'Always Becoming' Mindset

The phrase "always becoming" is a powerful antidote to the idea that by midlife we should have it all figured out. It rejects the notion of a fixed endpoint and instead embraces growth, curiosity, and reinvention as lifelong companions.

For women over 50, this mindset is not just refreshing, it is liberating.

Too often, women are told that midlife signals a plateau, that careers should wind down, or ambitions should shrink to fit someone else's expectations. But when you adopt the "always becoming" mindset, you claim your right to evolve at every stage. You recognise that you are not a finished product but a work of art in progress, layered, textured, and more interesting with every chapter.

According to celebrated psychologist Carl Jung, more people enter therapy around the age of 49 than at any other age.

Jung suggested that while young people should not be "too preoccupied with themselves," he added that it becomes a "duty and necessity" for aging persons to devote serious attention to themselves, implying that many people begin to seek deeper self-understanding, a core aspect of Jungian therapy in mid-life, around their 40s and 50s.

According to Jung, this period, often marked by an internal shift and a questioning of past achievements, is when individuals might feel a strong pull to connect with their authentic selves, leading them to pursue therapy to navigate this process of individuation.

Why midlife is a pivotal time for seeking therapy, according to Jung:

- **Internal Awakening:**
  In the 40s and beyond, the personality constructed around external achievements and societal approval may begin to feel hollow, leading to a search for a more authentic self.

- **Individuation:**
  Jung's concept of individuation, the process of becoming a whole and distinct individual, often intensifies in mid-life.

- **Integration of the Psyche:**
  This stage involves a significant inward turn, with individuals focusing on integrating different parts of their personality, including their conscious and unconscious selves, their inner child, and their "shadow" (the dark, hidden aspects of the personality).

- **"Duty and Necessity":**
  Jung stated that it is more of a "duty and necessity" for the aging person to focus on their inner world, contrasting it with the "sin" of preoccupation with self in youth.

What this means for therapy:

- Many people find themselves drawn to depth psychology (a term for Jungian and psychoanalytic therapies) during this "afternoon of life," as they seek to resolve inner conflicts and find deeper meaning in their lives.

- The process of therapy becomes a way to shed masks worn for the world and connect with one's genuine essence, particularly as life energy begins to wane and the need for a new way of living becomes apparent.

Women have a great advantage here because they are naturally drawn to compassion and empathy. By doing this deeper psychological work on yourself from 50 and beyond, you create a much smoother pathway for success and happiness in later years.

Practical Ways to Cultivate This Mindset

1. **Stay Curious:** Curiosity is the fuel for becoming. Take up a class, explore a hobby, or dive into a subject you know little about. Curiosity keeps the mind flexible and engaged.

2. **Challenge Old Stories:** Ask yourself what narratives you've inherited—"It's too late," "I'm not tech-savvy," "That ship has sailed." Then deliberately reframe them into empowering beliefs.

3. **Set Micro-Goals:** You don't need a five-year overhaul. Instead, set small goals, write for 15 minutes, network

with one new person, learn a new digital tool. Each step compounds.

4. **Surround Yourself with Expanders:** Connect with people who inspire you to stretch further, not shrink back. Their stories of reinvention will reinforce your own possibilities.

5. **Celebrate Progress, Not Perfection:** Becoming is messy, nonlinear, and beautiful. Instead of waiting for a "perfect outcome," acknowledge growth along the way.

The Deeper Reward

The "always becoming" mindset isn't about chasing endless achievements. It's about aligning your growth with meaning, purpose, and joy. It allows you to see aging not as a decline but as a widening horizon. Every year becomes an invitation to evolve, not into someone new, but into a fuller version of who you've always been.

Exercise: Create a Growth Plan

1. **Identify one area** where you feel you're slipping behind (digital tools, industry trends, networking).

2. **Write down one learning action** you can take this month (enroll in a short course, ask a colleague to show you a tool, attend a networking event).

3. **Set a resilience ritual** a daily or weekly habit that keeps you mentally strong (journaling, meditation, or gratitude practice).

Commit to reviewing your plan quarterly. Growth is not a one-time project; it's a lifelong practice.

Resources for Staying Current

Online Learning Platforms
- **Coursera** – University-level courses on everything from data science to leadership.
- **LinkedIn Learning** – Bite-sized courses on technology, communication, and professional development.
- **Udemy** – Affordable, wide-ranging courses, including personal growth, entrepreneurship, and digital skills.
- **edX** – Academic courses from institutions like Harvard and MIT, often free or low cost.
- **FutureLearn** – Courses with a strong global focus, including professional and personal development.

Podcasts & Thought Leaders

- **The Knowledge Project (Shane Parrish)** – Mental models, decision-making, and continuous learning.
- **The Long View (Morningstar)** – Finance and resilience through later career stages.
- **Women at Work (Harvard Business Review)** – Challenges and strategies for women navigating the workplace.
- **The Rich Roll Podcast** – Wellness, health, and personal transformation at any age.
- **Second Act Stories** – Real-life stories of midlife career change and reinvention.

Networking & Professional Groups

- **LinkedIn Groups** – Find niche communities relevant to your industry or stage of life.
- **Meetup** – Local and virtual groups for professional networking, learning, and hobbies.
- **Ellevate Network** – Global community for women professionals at all stages.
- **WISE (Women in Sports & Events), Women in Tech, Women in Business associations** – Industry-specific support.
- **Local Chambers of Commerce** – Great for small business owners and consultants.

Action Step: Choose one learning platform, one podcast, and one networking group from this list. Commit to exploring them within the next month as part of your Growth Plan.

Small, consistent steps will keep you both current and confident.

☄ Key Takeaways: Growth Mindset After 50

1. **Growth Mindset = Possibility**
   Believing that your skills, knowledge, and potential can continue to expand opens the door to new careers, hobbies, relationships, and ways of thinking.

2. **The Brain Still Learns**
   Neuroplasticity doesn't disappear with age. Your brain can still adapt and change, if you challenge it.

3. **Reframe the Question**
   Shift from asking *"What can I still do?"* to *"What do I want to do next?"* This simple pivot transforms limitation into opportunity.

4. **Small Steps = Big Change**
   You don't need to change everything at once. Consistent curiosity and small actions create momentum.

5. **Resilience Is Built, Not Inherited**
   Just like a growth mindset, resilience strengthens through practice, facing challenges, adapting, and moving forward with intention.

6. **Setbacks Become Stepping Stones**
   With a growth mindset, failure isn't the end, it's feedback. Resilient people use it to improve, not retreat.

7. **Emotional Flexibility Matters**
   After 50, resilience means adjusting to changes in identity, health, work, and relationships—while staying grounded and optimistic.

💡 CLAIRE'S TIP

"Stop asking if you're too old. Start asking what's still possible. The truth is, the only thing standing between you and your next chapter is the story you tell yourself. Choose one where you're still curious, still learning, and still evolving. Age doesn't close doors, mindset does. So keep that door wide open."

CONCLUSION

Your Next Act Is
Your Strongest

You've traveled through a lifetime of experiences, raising families, building careers, caring for others, navigating loss, and learning resilience in ways younger generations can't yet imagine. You've lived through eras of enormous social, cultural, and technological change. And now, at 50 and beyond, you stand at a rare and beautiful threshold. One that invites both reflection and reinvention.

This isn't an ending. It's an evolution.

For many women, midlife was once framed as a slow fade into invisibility. But this generation, *your* generation, is rewriting that story. We are seeing women rise to lead companies, launch businesses, join boards, write books, create art, mentor the next wave, and build financial and personal independence that will sustain them for decades to come.

You are not starting over, you are building forward with wisdom, clarity, and purpose. Every setback, every detour, every heartbreak has given you insight and strength. Those experiences are now your greatest assets.

The world doesn't need you to be younger, quieter, or smaller. It needs you to be visible, vibrant, and unapologetically present.

So, take what you've learned here, the frameworks, the reflections, the courage and build the next version of your life deliberately. Whether your next chapter is a business, a creative pursuit, a board role, or simply more time for what brings you peace, let it be a chapter that reflects who you have become, not who the world expected you to be.

Because success has no expiry date.
And your next act, crafted with intention, courage, and heart will be your strongest act yet.

References

Chapter 2: The Silent Saboteurs

- M. Scott Peck, The Road Less Traveled.
- Dr. Valerie Young, The Secret Thoughts of Successful Women: Why Capable People Suffer from Impostor Syndrome and How to Thrive in Spite of It.

Chapter 3: The Old Vision Wasn't Designed for You. It's Time to Write a New One

- Ada Calhoun, Why We Can't Sleep: Women's New Midlife Crisis.
- Chapter 5: From Gaps to Gateways: Turning Skills into Second-Act Power
- Simon Sinek, Start with Why.

Chapter 6: Professional Presence: The Makeover That Opens Doors

- Richard Bolles, What Colour is Your Parachute.
- Jane Evans, Invisible to Invaluable: Unleashing the Power of Midlife Women.

Chapter 7: The Power Web: Building and Using Networks That Elevate Life After 50

- Marti Barletta, Marketing To Women.
- Julia Gillard and Ngozi Okonjo-Iweala, Leadership: real lives, real lessons in 2020.

Chapter 14: Ageless Relevance: The Art of Staying Resilient in a Changing World

- Carol S. Dweck, Mindset.
- Brené Brown, Dare to Lead.
- Bill Burnett & Dave Evans, Designing Your Life.
- Tara Brach, Radical Acceptance.
- Sara Lawrence-Lightfoot, The Third Chapter.

Offer

Work With Claire —
Your Next Chapter Starts Here

Personalised Career Coaching for
Women Over 50

If this book has sparked something in you, a question, a longing, a quiet whisper that says "There's more for me" I would love to support you as you take the next steps.

I offer private career coaching for women over 50 who are ready to:

- Reclaim confidence and direction
- Redefine success on their own terms
- Explore new career paths, consulting, or business ideas
- Navigate ageism with strength and strategy
- Build a purposeful, financially confident next chapter

You don't have to do this alone. Together, we'll uncover your strengths, clarify your vision, map achievable goals, and create a personalised strategy that honours your experience, your values, and the life you want now.

My coaching is warm, practical, confidential, and designed specifically for women in midlife and beyond.

Whether you're returning to work, reinventing your career, launching something new, or simply longing for what's next, this is your invitation to step forward with support and clarity.

Ready to Begin?

Book a complimentary 20-minute discovery call to explore the possibilities and see if coaching with me is the right fit for you.

Visit: clairemoffat.com
Email: claire@clairemoffat.com

Your next act can be your strongest.

I'm here to help you make it happen.

Notes